HEALTHY EATING

HEALTHY EATING

BALANCED, NOURISHING
EVERYDAY RECIPES

Project Editor Siobhán O'Connor
Project Designer Alison Shackleton
Editors Kiron Gill, Megan Lea
US Editors Nathalie Mornu, Lori Hand
US Consultant Renee Wilmeth
Jacket Designer Alison Donovan
Jackets Coordinator Jasmin Lennie
Production Editor David Almond
Production Controller Denitsa Kenanska
Managing Editor Dawn Henderson
Managing Art Editor Alison Donovan
Art Director Maxine Pedliham
Publishing Director Katie Cowan

First American Edition, 2022
Published in the United States by DK Publishing
1450 Broadway, Suite 801, New York, NY 10018

Copyright © 2022 Dorling Kindersley Limited
DK, a Division of Penguin Random House LLC
22 23 24 25 26 10 9 8 7 6 5 4 3 2 1
001–326303–Mar/2022

A catalog record for this book is available from the Library of Congress.
ISBN 978-0-7440-5037-0

DK books are available at special discounts when purchased in bulk
for sales promotions, premiums, fund-raising, or educational use.
For details, contact: DK Publishing Special Markets, 1450 Broadway,
Suite 801, New York, NY 10018 SpecialSales@dk.com

Printed and bound in China

For the curious
www.dk.com

This book was made with Forest Stewardship Council ™ certified paper—
one small step in DK's commitment to a sustainable future.
For more information go to **www.dk.com/our-green-pledge**

Contents

Healthy

What we choose to fuel our bodies with affects not only our weight, but also our entire well-being. A good diet can be transformative: it can make us feel mentally alert and it helps our bodies function more efficiently. Most critically, it may protect us from the onset of chronic disease.

A holistic approach

Taking charge of our eating and cooking from scratch is often a good option for our wallets. Doing so should be viewed in a holistic way—think of it as savings banked to our health account that may work to cost us less in healthcare in the future.

A hectic life can mean that time is enemy number one when it comes to our food choices, often derailing us into making less nutritious ones. What we should be eating should be simple, right? Ironically, it is the constant barrage of mixed health information that can work in reverse, confusing us and making us lose sight of what normal eating is.

As scientists gain more insight into the unique properties of the foods we eat and how these fuel our bodies' nutritional needs and protect us against disease, nutritional guidelines provided by accredited dietary practitioners and government bodies shift in line with these new findings. What never changes, however, is the requirement to eat as many foods that are as close to nature as possible to nourish your body.

In the modern world where diets seem to be all about weight loss, it's easy to forget that we all need to eat really well to optimally nourish our bodies, boost vitality, and give us the best chance at great health—now and into the future.

Nature's whole food powerhouse

Rather than turning to supplements (although these have their place), you are almost always better off consuming the foods that provide these nutrients. In part this is because nature provides a wonderful balance and package of nutrients not found in individual supplements. In addition, plant foods provide a wealth of phytochemicals—substances such as antioxidants that benefit us enormously, way beyond our basic needs for vitamins and minerals.

There are particular foods that are the star players in providing nutrients and phytochemicals. These foods might be high in one particular nutrient, for example shellfish for their outstanding zinc content. Alternatively, a food may have a high level of a phytonutrient known to be beneficial in protecting against a particular disease.

Tomatoes are a good example because they provide a rich source of lycopene, shown to reduce the risk of prostate cancer in men. Other foods boast an army of protective phytochemicals and nutrients: Nuts are nutritional powerhouses providing many nutrients including fiber, folate, magnesium, vitamin E, riboflavin, calcium, and protein, along with a collection of different antioxidants. Extra virgin olive oil contains not just healthy, stable monounsaturated fat, but also vitamin E, at least 29 polyphenols (known to be protective in the body), a chemical called squalene that plays a role in protecting your skin from the sun, and a compound called oleocanthal that is anti-inflammatory. Foods such as these all have something extra to offer us.

The best news is that nutritious food does not have to be expensive or exotic. While there are certainly some really interesting foods that are imported from other areas of the world, including berries such as açai and goji, there are even more foods produced locally and available at your local fish market, butcher, or supermarket. Locally grown berries, broccoli, cabbage, watercress, Asian greens, mushrooms, seeds, oats, salmon, mussels, lean meats, and plain yogurt are just a few of the standout foods we can all fit more easily into our weekly menus. Look for budget-friendly hero foods too; canned salmon or mackerel, frozen berries, canned legumes, and packets of whole grains all help the family weekly budget go further.

How we fill our plates is also important. Your plate should be half-filled with colorful vegetables. Add to this a moderate amount of lean animal protein (eggs, chicken, beef, lamb, pork, or fish) and/or a plant-based one (tofu, tempeh, beans, or legumes), and a whole-grain carbohydrate (brown rice, barley, quinoa, and pastas made from pulses). While fats should make up a smaller part of our diet, they nonetheless have a key role to play in our health. Replace hydrogenated oils and saturated fats with moderate amounts of beneficial ones from nuts, seeds, olive oil, fatty fish, and avocados.

Taking the path toward better health

This book is designed to help you get more whole foods on your plate to boost your diet with nutrients. When you and your family eat well, you'll feel more energetic, you'll radiate better health, and you'll give your body the best protection you can against lifestyle-related diseases. Healthy food is attainable for everyone, via simple recipes created using an abundance of supermarket-sourced whole foods. In the mix are plenty of recipes that take 30 minutes or less; for winter months, there are recipes with brief preparation times that need a little longer to work their magic in the oven. Also included are wholesome recipes for entertaining or feeding a crowd, where you may want to make several dishes to share.

Above all we hope this book will inspire you to broaden the array of foods that you and your family consume, all put together in the most delicious but completely achievable way.

Healthy eating has never tasted so good!

LIGHT

Whether you are looking for a quick, satisfying lunch or inspiration for a light supper, you will find it here—all the benefits of whole foods without sacrificing flavor.

Chicken and egg salad with yogurt green goddess dressing

HIGH-PROTEIN | PREP + COOK TIME **25 MINUTES** | SERVES **4**

PER SERVING | Calories 835 | Carbohydrates 11g | Total sugars 8g | Fat 55g | Saturated fat 15g | Sodium 0.9g plus seasoning | Fiber 10g

The good fats in avocado give the vibrant green dressing used here a very luxurious texture and creamy taste. You can also try it with chargrilled meats, fish, or vegetables, or make it with half the amount of yogurt for a delicious dip.

1³/₄ lbs (800g) skinless, boneless chicken breast

2 garlic cloves, halved

4 eggs, room temperature

¹/₂ lb (200g) mixed cherry tomatoes, halved

¹/₂ cup firmly packed mint leaves

1¹/₂ cup celery stalks (about 3), thinly sliced

2 tbsp extra virgin olive oil

2 hearts of romaine, torn

3 avocados, sliced

¹/₃ cup sliced almonds, toasted

salt and freshly ground black pepper

green goddess dressing

2 cups spinach leaves

1¹/₂ cups firmly packed chopped mint leaves

1 avocado

1¹/₄ cups Greek yogurt

1 tbsp lemon juice

1 To make the green goddess dressing, place the spinach and mint in the bowl of a food processor. Pulse until finely chopped. Add the avocado, yogurt, and lemon juice; pulse until smooth. Season with salt and pepper to taste. Refrigerate until needed.

2 Fill a medium saucepan three-quarters full of cold water. Add the chicken and garlic, and bring to a boil. Reduce the heat to low; cook for 10 minutes or until the chicken is cooked through. Using a pair of tongs, transfer the chicken to a plate; set aside to cool. Discard the garlic.

3 Replace the water in the saucepan and bring to a boil. Add the eggs; cook for 6 minutes for soft-boiled. Drain and cool the eggs under cold running water. Peel the eggs, then cut in half.

4 Meanwhile, put the tomatoes and ¾ cup mint leaves in a large bowl; using a fork, crush the tomatoes slightly to release the juices. Add the celery and olive oil; toss to combine. Season with salt and pepper to taste.

5 Shred the poached chicken; divide the chicken, lettuce, tomato mixture, avocado and eggs evenly among 4 serving bowls. Drizzle with the tomato juices, and top each serving with some of the green goddess dressing. Serve sprinkled with the toasted almonds and remaining mint leaves.

Japanese-style tofu salad

VEGETARIAN | PREP + COOK TIME **30 MINUTES** | SERVES **4**

PER SERVING | Calories 685 | Carbohydrates 72g | Sugars 9g | Fat 29g | Saturated fat 5g | Sodium 2.7g plus seasoning | Fiber 9g

Silken tofu is produced without separating and pressing the soy curds, which results in a more delicate texture than other forms of tofu, so take care when cutting and coating it to preserve the shape. It also varies from soft to extra firm; firm silken tofu is used here.

16 oz (453 g) firm silken tofu, drained

2¹/₂ cups cooked brown and wild rice

1 cup frozen shelled edamame

¹/₂ cup pea shoots

1¹/₄ cups fresh asparagus, trimmed, thinly sliced lengthwise

4 green onions, white and light green parts, thinly sliced

¹/₄ cup pink pickled ginger, shredded

¹/₂ cup brown rice flour

sunflower oil for sautéing

2 nori sheets, finely shredded

1 tbsp sesame seeds, toasted

salt and freshly ground white pepper

soy dressing

¹/₄ cup light soy sauce

2 tbsp mirin

1 tbsp extra virgin olive oil

1 tbsp lime juice

1 Drain the tofu, and gently press it between paper towels to remove as much moisture as possible. Set aside.

2 To make the soy dressing, put the ingredients in a screw-top jar with a tight-fitting lid; shake well to combine.

3 Put the edamame in a large heatproof bowl; cover with boiling water. Let stand until thawed. Drain; cool under cold running water, then return to the bowl. Add the rice, pea shoots, asparagus, green onions, pickled ginger, and dressing; toss well to combine.

4 Cut the drained tofu into 1¹/₄ inch (3cm) pieces. Place in a large bowl with the rice flour; season with salt and white pepper to taste. Gently turn to coat, taking care not to break up the tofu.

5 Pour sunflower oil to a depth of ³/₄ inch (2cm) in a deep frying pan. Heat it over medium heat; sauté the tofu for 2 minutes on each side or until golden. Remove with a slotted spoon; drain on paper towels.

6 Divide the salad among 4 serving bowls; serve topped with the fried tofu, nori, and toasted sesame seeds.

TIP

Mirin, a sweet Japanese rice wine, is often paired with soy sauce in Japanese cooking. It is found in everything from marinades to ramen.

Steamed eggs with chile sauce

HIGH-PROTEIN | PREP + COOK TIME **55 MINUTES** | SERVES **4**

PER SERVING | Calories 458 | Carbohydrates 24g | Total sugars 9g | Fat 32g | Saturated fat 5g | Sodium 2.6g | Fiber 2g

Eggs provide very high-quality protein, with a near-perfect balance of the amino acids the human body needs. Scientific research is unequivocal in its support of higher protein diets for weight control, and eggs are a terrific food to boost the protein content of a meal.

8 x 6½ in (16 cm) rice paper rounds

extra virgin olive oil cooking spray

rice bran oil or other neutral oil like canola or olive oil for greasing the bowls

8 eggs

2 tsp sesame oil

5 cups baby spinach leaves

½ cup snow peas, thinly sliced

2 tsp black and white sesame seeds, toasted

1 cup Thai basil leaves

chile sauce

⅓ cup rice bran oil or other neutral oil

6 long red chiles, thinly sliced

1½ tbsp tamarind paste

1½ tbsp fish sauce

1½ tbsp grated dark palm sugar

1 tbsp light soy sauce

1 tbsp extra virgin olive oil

2 tsp tahini

1 tsp light brown sugar

1 To make the chile sauce, heat the rice bran oil in a small saucepan over medium heat; cook the chile, stirring occasionally, for 3 minutes or until soft. Remove from the heat; stir in the remaining ingredients, and mix well to combine. Set aside to cool.

2 Spray 1 rice paper round with a little of the olive oil; microwave on high (100%) for 50 seconds or until puffed up and white. Repeat with the remaining rice papers. Set aside.

3 Place a larger bamboo steamer over a large wok of boiling water. Grease four 1½–cup (375ml) ceramic dishes or rice bowls with a little rice bran oil. Crack 2 eggs into each bowl. Carefully place the bowls in the steamer; steam, covered, for 5–8 minutes until the whites of the eggs are set but the yolks remain runny. (The cooking time of the eggs will vary depending on the depth of the bowls.)

4 Meanwhile, heat the sesame oil in a frying pan over medium heat; cook the spinach, stirring, for 2 minutes or until wilted. Remove the spinach from the pan; combine with the snow peas and 1 tablespoon water, and toss for 1 minute or until bright green.

5 Top the eggs with the wilted spinach, snow peas, sesame seeds, basil leaves, and chile sauce. Serve with the rice paper crisps.

TIP

The heat of chiles varies. If you'd like a milder sauce, seed half of the chiles before slicing.

Double broccoli pizza

HIGH-FIBER | PREP + COOK TIME **1 HOUR** | SERVES **4**

PER SERVING | Calories 377 | Carbohydrates 12g | Total sugars 8g | Fat 21g | Saturated fat 9g | Sodium 1.2g plus seasoning | Fiber 14g

Broccoli is a part of the *Brassica* genus, which is noted for its high vitamin A, C, E folate, and potassium content. What makes brassicas special, however, is a group of antioxidants called flavonoids. These act as anti-cancer agents and ramp up detoxifying enzyme systems.

2 lb (1 kg) broccoli (about 3 full heads), trimmed, cut into florets (see tip)

1/4 cup grated Cheddar cheese

1 egg, lightly beaten

1/4 cup finely grated Parmesan cheese, plus extra for serving

1/2 cup prepared pizza sauce

3/4 lb (340g) broccolini, trimmed

2 tbsp extra virgin olive oil

3 1/2 oz (100g) buffalo mozzarella, torn

1/2 cup pitted green olives, halved

salt and freshly ground black pepper

1 Preheat the oven to 400°F (200°C). Line two baking sheets with parchment paper.

2 In a food processor, add the broccoli florets and pulse until finely chopped. Transfer to a microwave-safe bowl, and cover with plastic wrap; microwave on high (100%) for 12 minutes or until tender. Drain, then allow to cool slightly. Put the broccoli in the center of a clean kitchen towel or cheese cloth. Gather the ends of the towel or cheese cloth together, then squeeze out as much liquid as possible.

3 Combine the broccoli, Cheddar cheese, egg, and 1/4 cup of the Parmesan cheese in a bowl; season with salt and pepper to taste. Divide the mixture evenly between the prepared trays, pressing each portion into an 8 inch (22cm) round.

4 Bake the pizza bases for 25 minutes or until golden. Spread each base with pizza sauce, leaving a 3/4 inch (2cm) border around the edge. Top with the broccolini, cutting any thick stems in half lengthwise. Drizzle with olive oil, and bake for 10 minutes longer.

5 Top the pizza with the mozzarella and green olives. Bake for 10 minutes longer or until the cheese is melted and the broccoli tender. Serve sprinkled with the remaining Parmesan cheese.

TIPS

- When trimming florets, don't discard the broccoli stems. Save them for another recipe like the nori crunch salad on page 21.
- Make this recipe vegetarian by using a vegetarian hard cheese instead of Parmesan cheese.

Farmers market bowl

VEGETARIAN | PREP + COOK TIME **35 MINUTES** | SERVES **4**
PER SERVING | Calories 413 | Carbohydrates 30g | Total sugars 17g | Fat 19g | Saturated fat 6g | Sodium 1.2g plus seasoning | Fiber 12g

Brussels sprouts contain several powerful flavonoids; they also contain large amounts
of vitamin K, which is thought to prevent or at least delay the onset of Alzheimer's disease.
Buckwheat, which is similar to quinoa, is a good source of fiber and complex carbohydrates.

14 oz (400g) brussels sprouts, sliced

1 lb (450g) mixed heirloom baby carrots,
 trimmed, halved lengthwise

1 lb (450g) small pattypan squash

4 tbsp extra virgin olive oil, divided

1/4 lb (125g) kale, trimmed

1/4 cup raw buckwheat (see tips)

2 tsp tamari

4 eggs

salt and freshly ground black pepper

harissa labneh

1/2 cup roasted peppers, drained if from a jar

2 tsp harissa paste

1 tbsp red wine vinegar

1 1/2 cups labneh (see tips)

1 To make the harissa labneh, process or blend the roasted peppers with
   the harissa and vinegar. Stir one-quarter of the harissa mixture through
   the labneh in large swirls. Set aside both the labneh and the remaining
   harissa mixture.

2 Preheat the oven to 425°F (220°C). Line 2 baking sheets with parchment
   paper.

3 Arrange the Brussels sprouts, carrots, and pattypan squash in 3 rows
   on one of the baking trays. Drizzle with 1 tablespoon of the olive oil;
   season with salt and pepper to taste. Roast for 20 minutes or until the
   vegetables are just tender and starting to brown around the edges.

4 Place the kale on one side of the remaining tray; drizzle with 1 tablespoon
   of the olive oil, and toss to combine. Put the buckwheat on the other side
   of the tray; drizzle with the tamari, and stir to combine. Bake at the same
   time as the vegetables for 8 minutes or until the buckwheat is dry and
   the kale is crisp.

5 Meanwhile, heat the remaining olive oil in a large, nonstick frying pan
   over high heat. Crack the eggs into the pan, one at a time; cook for
   2 minutes or until the whites are set, the edges are crisp, and the yolks
   are cooked to your liking.

6 Spread the harissa labneh over the bottom of 4 shallow serving bowls.
   Divide the vegetables and eggs evenly among the bowls. Sprinkle with
   the tamari buckwheat. Serve with the remaining harissa mixture.

TIPS

• Instead of the roasted buckwheat, you can use
chopped tamari roasted almonds or a purchased
mix of toasted seeds, if you like.

• Thick and tangy, labneh is almost like soft cream
cheese. Use Greek yogurt if you prefer. Simply strain
it through a cheese cloth to remove the excess whey.

Japanese oat and nori crunch salad

VEGETARIAN | PREP **30 MINUTES** | SERVES **4**

PER SERVING | Calories 615 | Carbohydrates 18g | Total sugars 9g | Fat 50g | Saturated fat 9g | Sodium 1.5g plus seasoning | Fiber 14g

If you're preparing this salad ahead of time to enjoy later, pack the nori crunch and miso dressing into separate small containers and the salad into a larger one to transport. Assemble the salad just before eating for maximum crunch and zing.

1 large carrot, shredded

2 medium beets, peeled and shredded

3 broccoli stalks, peeled and julienned

1 cup coarsely chopped mint leaves

4 cups kale

4 avocados

1/2 cup blanched almonds, toasted

nori crunch

1 tbsp sesame oil

2 garlic cloves, crushed

1 tbsp white miso (shiro miso)

2 nori sheets, finely shredded

2 tbsp pumpkin seeds, finely chopped

1/4 cup rolled (old fashioned) oats

1/2 cup firmly packed coarsely chopped kale

salt and freshly ground black pepper

miso dressing

2 tbsp white miso (shiro miso)

2 tsp sesame oil

1/4 cup apple cider vinegar

1 large garlic clove, crushed

1 tsp pure maple syrup

TIP

Nori is the seaweed used for sushi rolls. You can find it in the Asian section of your grocery store.

1 To make the nori crunch, preheat the oven to 325°F (160°C). Line a large baking sheet with parchment paper. Combine the sesame oil, garlic, white miso, nori, and 1 tablespoon water in a large bowl. Next, add the pumpkin seeds, oats, and chopped kale; toss well to combine. Season with salt and pepper to taste. Spread the mixture over the prepared tray; bake for 20 minutes or until golden, turning halfway during the cooking time. Set aside to cool.

2 To make the miso dressing, put all the ingredients and 1 tablespoon water in a screw-top jar with a tight-fitting lid; shake well to combine. Season with salt and pepper to taste.

3 Put the carrots, beets, broccoli stalks, and mint in a large bowl; add a third of the dressing, and toss to combine. Divide evenly among 4 serving bowls. Combine the kale with another third of the dressing; divide among the serving bowls. Remove the pits from each avocado and evenly divide between each serving. Drizzle the avocados with the remaining dressing. Serve the salad scattered with the nori crunch and toasted almonds.

Chicken and brown rice larb cups

FAST | PREP + COOK TIME **20 MINUTES** | SERVES **4**

PER SERVING | Calories 432 | Carbohydrates 41g | Total sugars 3g | Fat 13g | Saturated fat 3g | Sodium 2.4g | Fiber 4g

Larb is a tangy salad of ground chicken (or pork) and fresh herbs, originating from Laos, but also found in northern Thailand. This version keeps the traditional flavors but mixes them with brown and wild rice for extra fiber.

3 cups cooked brown and wild rice

1 tbsp extra virgin olive oil

1 lb (450g) ground chicken

4 green onions, thinly sliced

1/3 cup cilantro, finely chopped, plus extra leaves for serving

2 garlic cloves, crushed

2 tsp grated ginger

2 tbsp fish sauce

2 tbsp lime juice

4 makrut lime leaves, finely shredded

2 romaine hearts, leaves separated

1/3 cup roasted unsalted cashews, chopped

1 cucumber, seeded, finely chopped

1 long red chile, thinly sliced lengthways

lime wedges, for serving

1 Heat the olive oil in a large wok over high heat; stir-fry the chicken for 4 minutes, breaking up any lumps. Add the green onions, chopped cilantro, garlic, ginger, and rice; stir-fry for 1 minute or until combined. Next, add the fish sauce, lime juice, and makrut lime leaves; continue stir-frying until just combined.

2 Divide the chicken mixture among the lettuce leaves. Top with the roasted cashews, cucumber, chile, and extra cilantro leaves. Serve with the lime wedges for squeezing over.

Chargrilled sides

These flavor-packed sides are stars in their own right, turning the notion of worthy but dull vegetable accompaniments on its head. Quick chargrilling helps to preserve nutrients and color, and each dish can be used to expand a meal into a more substantial offering.

Hoisin eggplant

PREP + COOK TIME **20 MINUTES** | SERVES **4**

Preheat a ridged cast-iron grill pan over high heat. Cut 3 eggplants into 2 inch (5mm) rounds on a slight diagonal. Brush the eggplant slices with 1 cup hoisin sauce, then spray with extra virgin olive oil. Cook the eggplant, in batches, for 4 minutes on each side or until tender and grill marks appear. Arrange the eggplant slices on a platter. For the dressing, whisk together 1/2 cup tamari, 2 tablespoons light brown sugar, and 1 teaspoon sesame oil; drizzle over the eggplant. Sprinkle with 2 teaspoons toasted sesame seeds, 2 tablespoons fried shallots, and 1 finely sliced long red chile.

Zucchini and dukkah

PREP + COOK TIME **20 MINUTES** | SERVES **4**

Cut 6 zucchini or summer squash into four lengthwise. Toss in a large bowl with 2 tablespoons extra virgin olive oil. Heat a ridged cast-iron grill pan over medium heat; cook the zucchini, in two batches, for 3 minutes on each side or until grill marks appear. Toss the zucchini with 1 teaspoon honey and 2 tablespoons dukkah to coat. Split 1 whole-grain pita bread in half. Spray with extra virgin olive oil; chargrill for 1 minute on each side until crisp. Serve the bread crumbled over the zucchini with 1/2 cup crumbled feta cheese.

Sweet pepper salad

PREP + COOK TIME **30 MINUTES** | SERVES **4**

Preheat a ridged cast-iron grill pan over high heat. Slice 2 red onions into 1/4 inch (5 mm) thick slices. Brush with olive oil; chargrill for 1 minute on each side or until slightly softened. Place on a serving platter. Halve, seed, and cut 3/4 lb (350g) bell peppers and sweet peppers into thick slices. Coat with olive oil; chargrill for 90 seconds on each side or until just tender. Add 8 oz (220g) cherry tomatoes, halved, to the platter. Combine 2 tablespoons extra virgin olive oil with 1 1/2 tablespoons lemon juice; drizzle over the vegetables. Sprinkle with 1/3 cup toasted pine nuts and 8 oz (220g) bocconcini cheese (fresh mozzarella pearls), torn in half.

Lemony chili asparagus

PREP + COOK TIME **20 MINUTES** | SERVES **4**

Preheat a ridged cast-iron grill pan over high heat. Trim 3/4 inch (2cm) from the ends of 1 lb (450g) asparagus. Group the asparagus spears in threes, side by side, then thread 2 toothpicks or metal skewers through each group to hold them together. Brush the asparagus with 2 tablespoons chili-infused olive oil. Chargrill for 2 minutes on each side until tender. Serve with arugula, finely grated Parmesan cheese, and lemon wedges for squeezing over.

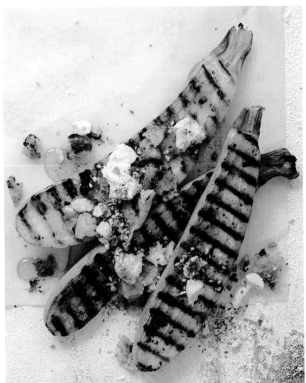

Thai-style fried rice

FAST | PREP + COOK TIME **35 MINUTES** | SERVES **4**

PER SERVING | Calories 423 | Carbohydrates 40g | Total sugars 5g | Fat 14g | Saturated fat 3g | Sodium 3.5g | Fiber 3g

You can make this fried rice with chicken by substituting the shrimp with 1lb (450g) shredded cooked skinless boneless chicken breast. Cook your own rice or use pre-cooked brown rice from the store. Fried rice is also a great way to use up leftover rice from another meal.

3 cups cooked brown, red, and wild rice mix

2 tbsp extra virgin olive oil, divided

4 eggs, lightly beaten

4 shallots, thinly sliced

2 tbsp Thai red curry paste

2 garlic cloves, crushed

1lb (450g) uncooked shrimp, peeled and deveined, tails intact

5oz (150g) mixed Asian mushrooms such as oyster and shiitake

1 red bell pepper, thinly sliced

2 tbsp light soy sauce

1 tbsp fish sauce

1 tbsp lime juice

1 cup Thai basil leaves

lime wedges, for serving (optional)

1 If using packaged brown rice, heat it according to the package instructions.

2 Meanwhile, heat 1 tablespoon of the olive oil in a large, nonstick wok over high heat. Add the beaten eggs, swirling the pan slightly to create an omelette about 8in (20cm) in diameter. Using a spatula, pull the egg inward from the edge of the wok toward the center to create folds, letting the uncooked egg mixture fill any gaps. Cook for 3 minutes or until set. Still using the spatula, roll up the omelette in the wok, then slide it carefully onto a board; cut into 1/2in (1cm) thick slices. Set aside.

3 Heat the remaining olive oil in the same wok over high heat; stir-fry the shallots for 3 minutes or until softened. Add the curry paste and garlic; stir-fry for 30 seconds until fragrant.

4 Add the shrimp, mushrooms, and red bell pepper; stir-fry for 4 minutes or until cooked through.

5 Add the rice and cooked egg; stir-fry for 1 minute until heated through. Stir in the soy and fish sauces, lime juice, and basil leaves. Serve with lime wedges for squeezing over, if you like.

Roasted broccolini, edamame, and chile tempeh salad

FAST | PREP + COOK TIME **25 MINUTES** | SERVES **4**

PER SERVING | Calories 390 | Carbohydrates 20g | Total sugars 9.5g | Fat 20g | Saturated fat 3g | Sodium 1.1g plus seasoning | Fiber 12g

The chemical responsible for the heat of a spicy chile is capsaicin. This fiery compound has many potential health benefits, including heart health, pain relief, and weight loss. It also increases the body's production of heat and can help to clear nasal congestion.

8 oz (227g) chickpea tempeh

1 tbsp tamari

1 tbsp honey

2 long red chiles, chopped, divided

3/4 lb (350g) broccolini, trimmed

2 cups frozen shelled edamame

2 tbsp peanut oil

1/2 lb (240g) mixed salad leaves

salt and freshly ground black pepper

lime halves, for serving

cashew dressing

2 tbsp cashew butter

1 1/2 tbsp lime juice

1 tbsp tamari

1 tbsp peanut oil

1 Preheat the oven to 400°F (200°C). Line two large baking sheets with parchment paper.

2 Using your hands, gently crumble the tempeh into a bowl, forming a mixture of large and small chunks. Add the tamari, honey, and half of the chopped chiles; toss gently to combine. Spread the mixture over one of the prepared baking sheets.

3 Put the broccolini and edamame on the remaining baking sheet; drizzle with peanut oil, then toss the vegetables to coat. Season with salt and pepper to taste. Roast in the oven for 15 minutes or until the broccolini is just tender and the tempeh is golden.

4 Meanwhile, to make the cashew dressing, place the ingredients together in a screw-top jar with a tight-fitting lid. Add 1 tablespoon of cold water. Shake well to combine. Add an extra tablespoon of cold water to thin, if needed.

5 Arrange the roasted broccolini, edamame, and salad leaves in a large bowl; toss gently. Divide evenly among 4 serving plates. Top with the tempeh, and drizzle with the cashew dressing. Scatter the remaining chiles on top. Serve with lime halves for squeezing over.

Bang bang salmon salad

HIGH-PROTEIN | PREP + COOK TIME **30 MINUTES** | SERVES **4**

PER SERVING | Calories 539 | Carbohydrates 16g | Total sugars 7g | Fat 37g | Saturated fat 7g | Sodium 0.8g | Fiber 6g

Salmon takes the place of chicken in this version of the classic Szechuan street food, with its fiery dressing characteristic of the regional Chinese cuisine. If you don't have a microwave, serve the salmon with steamed brown rice or quinoa instead of the rice paper crisps.

1 tbsp extra virgin olive oil

2 x $\frac{1}{2}$ lb (250g) skinless salmon fillets

2 carrots, julienned

2 cucumbers, seeded, julienned

$\frac{1}{2}$ cup pea shoots

4 green onions, thinly sliced lengthwise

1 cup cilantro leaves

4 x 6$\frac{1}{2}$ in (17 cm) rice paper rounds

extra virgin olive oil cooking spray

2 tbsp sesame seeds, toasted

lime wedges, for serving (optional)

bang bang dressing

1 tsp Szechuan peppercorns

$\frac{1}{2}$ tsp dried chili flakes

$\frac{1}{4}$ cup sesame seeds

2 tbsp Chinese black vinegar

1 tbsp light soy sauce

1 tbsp extra virgin olive oil

2 tsp tahini

1 tsp light brown sugar

1 Heat the olive oil in a large frying pan over high heat. Cook the salmon for 4 minutes; turn and cook on the other side for 2 minutes longer or until just cooked and still pink in the center. Set aside.

2 Gently toss the carrots, cucumbers, pea shoots, green onions, and cilantro leaves in a large bowl.

3 To make the bang bang dressing, stir the Szechuan peppercorns, chili flakes, and sesame seeds in a small frying pan over medium heat for 2 minutes or until the seeds are toasted; be careful not to scorch. Allow to cool, then grind to a fine powder using a spice mill or a mortar and pestle. Put in a screw-top jar with a tight-fitting lid. Add the remaining dressing ingredients; shake well to combine.

4 Spray 1 rice paper round with a little of the olive oil; microwave on high (100%) for 50 seconds or until puffed up and white. Repeat with the remaining rice papers.

5 Using a fork, flake the salmon into large pieces. Put in a bowl with the bang bang dressing; toss gently to coat the salmon with the dressing. Arrange the carrot mixture on a platter; top with the salmon.

6 Sprinkle the bang bang salmon with the toasted sesame seeds. Serve with the rice paper crisps and lime wedges for squeezing over, if you like.

TIP

You can shred the carrot with a julienne peeler, mandoline, or V-slicer. If you don't own any of these, coarsely grate the carrot instead.

Couscous and haloumi cheese salad with smoky tomato dressing

FAST | PREP **25 MINUTES** | SERVES **4**

PER SERVING | Calories 576 | Carbohydrates 59g | Total sugars 10g | Fat 22g | Saturated fat 11g | Sodium 2.3g plus seasoning | Fiber 15g

The carbohydrates in beans, peas, and lentils are absorbed very slowly, giving pulses low glycemic index (GI) values—this makes them very good at filling you up. Low-GI foods are those with a score of 55 or less. Chickpeas, for example, have a GI of 36.

1 cup whole-grain pearl couscous

1 x 15 oz (425g) can chickpeas, drained, rinsed

2 zucchinis, julienned

8 oz (225g) mixed cherry tomatoes, halved

2 tsp extra virgin olive oil

8 oz (225g) haloumi cheese, cut into $3/4$ in (2cm) pieces

$1/4$ cup dukkah

$1/2$ cup cilantro leaves, for serving

smoky tomato dressing

1 tbsp extra virgin olive oil

8 oz (225g) mixed cherry tomatoes, quartered

1 small red onion, finely chopped

8 oz (125g) jar pimentos, drained, finely chopped

1 tsp smoked paprika

$1/4$ cup red wine vinegar

salt and freshly ground black pepper

1 To make the smoky tomato dressing, heat the olive oil in a medium nonstick frying pan over medium heat. Cook the tomatoes, onion, pimentos, and paprika, stirring, for 4 minutes or until the tomatoes start to release their juices. Stir in the vinegar. Remove from the heat; season with salt and pepper to taste. Set aside to cool.

2 Cook the couscous in a medium saucepan of salted boiling water over high heat for 6 minutes or until tender; drain. Place the couscous in a large bowl with the chickpeas, zucchini, tomatoes, and the smoky tomato dressing.

3 Heat the olive oil in a large nonstick frying pan over high heat. Cook the haloumi cheese for 2 minutes on each side or until golden. Add the dukkah, and toss to coat the cheese.

4 Add the haloumi cheese to the salad; toss gently to mix. Serve topped with the cilantro.

TIP

You can slice the zucchini with a julienne peeler, mandoline, or V-slicer. If you don't have one, coarsely grate them instead.

Loaded avocados with bulgur wheat

FAST | PREP + COOK TIME **15 MINUTES + STANDING** | SERVES **4**

PER SERVING | Calories 642 | Carbohydrates 19g | Total sugars 3g | Fat 54g | Saturated fat 16g | Sodium 0.6g plus seasoning | Fiber 9g

Whole-grain bulgur wheat, used for centuries in Middle Eastern cuisine, is high in fiber and has a high manganese content. An essential nutrient, manganese aids calcium absorption in our bodies. It is also vital for normal nerve and brain function.

1/2 cup coarse bulgur wheat

4 avocados

3 green onions, coarsely chopped

1/2 cup small basil leaves

8 oz (225g) small mozzarella balls, torn

4 oz (125g) heirloom cherry tomatoes, halved

salt and freshly ground black pepper

lemony dressing

1/4 cup extra virgin olive oil

2 tbsp lemon juice

1 garlic clove, crushed

1 Put the bulgur wheat in a medium bowl; cover with boiling water. Let stand for 10 minutes or until the grains are swollen and tender. Drain well and set aside.

2 To make the lemony dressing, put the dressing ingredients in a screw-top jar with a tight-fitting lid; shake well to combine. Season with salt and pepper to taste.

3 Cut each avocado in half and remove the pits. Using a spoon, scoop out large chunks of the flesh from the avocado, reserving the avocado shells with the skin intact.

4 Put the soaked bulgur wheat, scooped avocado, green onions, basil, mozzarella balls, and tomatoes in a large bowl. Drizzle with the lemony dressing; season with salt and pepper to taste. Mix gently. Spoon the bulgur mixture into the avocado shells. Serve immediately.

TIP

You could use 1/2 cup whole-grain couscous instead of the bulgur wheat. To cook it, put the couscous in a small heatproof bowl; cover with 1/2 cup boiling water. Cover the bowl tightly with plastic wrap. Let stand for 5 minutes, then fluff the couscous grains with a fork.

Green quinoa and chicken salad

PORTABLE | PREP + COOK TIME **40 MINUTES + REFRIGERATION** | SERVES **4**

PER SERVING | Calories 651 | Carbohydrates 31g | Total sugars 6g | Fat 42g | Saturated fat 7g | Sodium 0.3g plus seasoning | Fiber 8g

Although quinoa is cooked and eaten as a grain alternative, it is in fact a seed. While many of us might consider it relatively new to the pantry, quinoa has been a staple food for thousands of years in the Andean region of South America. The Incas reportedly considered it sacred, calling it the "mother of all grains."

2 x 6 oz (200g) skinless boneless chicken breasts

4 garlic cloves, thinly sliced

½ cup extra virgin olive oil

3 tsp finely grated lemon zest

½ cup lemon juice

¼ cup oregano

4 cups baby spinach leaves, divided

1 cup white quinoa

2 avocados

8 oz (225g) heirloom cherry tomatoes, halved

1 cucumber, thinly sliced lengthwise into ribbons

salt and freshly ground black pepper

1 Cut each chicken breast in half horizontally to make 4 thinner fillets. Place in a glass or stainless-steel bowl with the garlic.

2 Whisk together the olive oil, lemon zest and juice, and oregano in a small bowl. Pour ¼ cup of the dressing over the chicken; turn to coat well. Cover and refrigerate for 20 minutes.

3 Meanwhile, in the bowl of a food processor, combine the remaining dressing with 1 cup of the spinach leaves. Pulse until smooth. Season with salt and pepper to taste. Set aside.

4 Put the quinoa in a fine strainer; rinse under cold running water until the water runs clear. Place the drained quinoa into a medium saucepan. Add 2 cups water; bring to a boil. Cook, covered, for 15 minutes. Remove from the heat; let stand, covered, for 5 minutes. Fluff the grains with a fork.

5 Meanwhile, heat a ridged cast-iron grill pan over high heat; cook the chicken for 5 minutes on each side, or until cooked through and grill marks appear. Allow to rest, loosely covered with aluminum foil, for 5 minutes, then cut diagonally into ¾ inch (2cm) thick slices.

6 Cut the avocados in half and remove the pits. Scoop out the flesh from the avocado using a spoon. Put the quinoa in a large bowl with the spinach dressing; toss to combine. Season with salt and pepper to taste. Add the remaining spinach, avocado, tomatoes, and cucumber; toss. Serve the salad topped with the sliced chicken.

Supergreens Spanish omelette

HIGH-PROTEIN | PREP + COOK TIME **55 MINUTES + STANDING** | SERVES **4**
PER SERVING | Calories 429 | Carbohydrates 23g | Total sugars 2g | Fat 24g | Saturated fat 7g | Sodium 0.8g plus seasoning | Fiber 4g

Leafy greens are without a doubt one of the top foods to include in your daily diet.
They are among the most nutrient-dense foods, yet contain very few calories, and they're
anti-inflammatory. Curly kale definitely falls into this category. Not only is it a great source
of vitamin C, but it contains phytonutrients that help to support eye health as well.

³/₄ lb (440g) potatoes, cut into ¹/₂ in (1.5cm) cubes

1 tsp smoked paprika

2 tbsp extra virgin olive oil, divided

3 cups shredded curly kale

10 eggs

extra virgin olive oil cooking spray

¹/₂ cup frozen peas, thawed

1¹/₂ oz (50g) grated pecorino cheese or
Parmesan cheese

salt and freshly ground black pepper

1   Preheat the oven to 350°F (180°C). Line a large baking sheet with
    parchment paper.

2   Toss the potatoes with the paprika and 1 tbsp of the olive oil on the
    prepared baking sheet; season with salt and pepper to taste. Put the
    kale in a medium bowl; drizzle with the remaining oil. Using your
    fingertips, massage the oil into the kale to coat.

3   Bake the potatoes for 15 minutes; add the kale to the baking sheet,
    setting aside the bowl to reuse in the next step. Bake for 10 minutes
    longer or until the potatoes are tender.

4   Lightly whisk the eggs in the bowl; season with salt and pepper to taste.
    Spray a 10 inch (25cm) nonstick ovenproof skillet with the olive oil
    cooking spray. Heat over medium heat. Sprinkle the potatoes, kale, and
    peas over the bottom of the pan. Pour the egg mixture over top; cook for
    2 minutes or until the egg is starting to set and pull away from the edge
    of the pan. Transfer the omelette, still in the pan, to the oven; cook for
    15 minutes or until the egg is just set in the center.

5   Leave the omelette to cool slightly before removing from the pan.
    Sprinkle the pecorino cheese over the top, and cut into wedges to serve.

TIPS

- Refrigerate any leftovers for easy school or work
lunches, or chop as "croutons" to toss over a salad.
- Try a bunch of chopped fresh asparagus instead
of the peas. Parmesan, feta, ricotta, or aged Cheddar
cheeses can all be used instead of the pecorino
cheese, if you like.

Jalapeño steak and watermelon salad

HIGH-PROTEIN | PREP + COOK TIME **25 MINUTES** | SERVES **4**

PER SERVING | Calories 614 | Carbohydrates 89g | Total sugars 82g | Fat 25g | Saturated fat 5g | Sodium 0.5g plus seasoning | Fiber 7g

Red meat is rich in zinc, a mineral often typically low in diets. Zinc is essential for immune function; that's why you'll find it added to cold and flu remedies. Eating red meat a few times a week is all you need to significantly boost the zinc in your diet.

1 lb (450g) beef flank or flat iron steaks

2 tbsp pickled sliced jalapeños, plus ⅓ cup pickling liquid, divided

2 tbsp extra virgin olive oil, divided

2 avocados, divided

1 head iceberg lettuce, cut into 10 wedges

1½ cups firmly packed mint leaves, divided

1 tbsp lime juice

2–3 lb (1kg) seedless watermelon, rind removed, thinly sliced

1 tbsp black and white sesame seeds, toasted

salt and freshly ground black pepper

lime wedges, to serve

1 Put the steaks in a bowl with half of the jalapeño pickling liquid and 1 tablespoon of the oil, making sure the meat is coated in liquid. Season well with salt and a good grinding of pepper. Let sit for 10 minutes.

2 Cut 1 avocado in half and remove the pit. Using a spoon, scoop the flesh into the bowl of a food processor. Add 1 lettuce wedge, ½ cup mint, lime juice, remaining pickling liquid, and remaining olive oil. Process until smooth; season with salt and pepper to taste. Set aside.

3 Heat a ridged cast-iron grill pan to high heat. Cook the steaks for 3 minutes on one side or until grill marks appear; turn and cook for 3 minutes longer for medium rare or until cooked to your liking. Let rest for 5 minutes, loosely covered with aluminum foil.

4 Spread three-quarters of the avocado dressing over the bottom of a large, shallow platter; top with the remaining lettuce and mint, as well as the watermelon. Thinly slice the steak and arrange on the salad; scatter with the jalapeños, and sprinkle the toasted sesame seeds over top. Lastly, top with the remaining avocado, cut into wedges. Serve with the rest of the dressing and lime wedges for squeezing over.

Thai salmon and chia fishcakes with watercress salad

HIGH-PROTEIN | PREP **20 MINUTES** | SERVES **4**

PER SERVING | Calories 606 | Carbohydrates 6g | Total sugars 2g | Fat 42g | Saturated fat 7g | Sodium 1.6g plus seasoning | Fiber 7g

Salmon fishcakes can be a great way to ensure dietary intake of omega-3 fatty acids, which are essential for brain health. Chia seeds also contain omega-3, which can lower blood pressure. In these fishcakes, the fragrant Thai flavors of ginger, coriander, and lime shine.

1/4 cup black chia seeds

1 tbsp grated ginger

1/4 cup finely chopped cilantro

1 shallot, finely chopped

2 tsp finely grated lime zest

2 tsp fish sauce

1 3/4 lb (800g) skinless salmon fillets, cut into 1/2 in (2cm) pieces

2 tbsp extra virgin olive oil, divided

salt and freshly ground black pepper

watercress salad

1 cucumber, thinly sliced into ribbons

4 cups watercress, washed, trimmed

1 cup cilantro leaves

1 shallot, halved, thinly sliced

1 tsp grated ginger

1 long green chile, finely chopped

2 tbsp lime juice

2 tsp fish sauce

1 tbsp extra virgin olive oil

1 Stir together the chia seeds and 1/2 cup warm water in a small bowl. Let stand for 5 minutes to soak.

2 In the bowl of a food processor, add the ginger, cilantro, shallot, lime zest, fish sauce, and chia seeds. Process until just combined. Add the salmon; pulse until combined. Season well with salt and a good grinding of pepper.

3 Divide the mixture into twelve 1/3-cup portions. Flatten into 3 inch (8cm) rounds. Place on a baking sheet lined with parchment paper; refrigerate for 20 minutes to firm slightly.

4 Meanwhile, to make the watercress salad, put the cucumber, watercress, and cilantro leaves in a large bowl; toss. Put the shallot, ginger, chile, lime juice, fish sauce, and olive oil in a screw-top jar with a tight-fitting lid; shake well. Drizzle half of the dressing over the salad, then toss to mix evenly; reserve the remaining dressing to serve.

5 Heat 1 tablespoon of the olive oil in a large nonstick frying pan over high heat. Cook half of the fishcakes for 2 minutes on each side or until browned and cooked through. Transfer to a tray; cover to keep warm. Repeat with the remaining oil and fishcakes.

6 Divide the watercress salad evenly among 4 serving plates. Add 3 fishcakes to each plate, placing them beside the salad. Drizzle the remaining dressing over the fish. Serve immediately.

Lemony chicken and kale broth

HIGH-PROTEIN | PREP + COOK TIME **40 MINUTES** | SERVES **4**

PER SERVING | Calories 438 | Carbohydrates 44g | Total sugars 4g | Fat 11g | Saturated fat 2g | Sodium 0.8g | Fiber 5g

Chicken provides more iron and zinc in the leg and thigh meat, which is why thigh fillets are used in this broth instead of breast meat. They are also more flavorful. Plus you'll benefit from a boost of B group vitamins, with niacin as the star player. Lemons and lemon juice contain a range of phytochemicals, including flavonoids.

2 tbsp extra virgin olive oil, divided

4 green onions, sliced, green ends reserved

2 garlic cloves, sliced

1¼ lb (600g) boneless chicken thighs, cut into 2in (5cm) pieces

12 baby new potatoes, halved

4 cups vegetable stock

4 x ¼ in (6mm) thick slices of sourdough bread

1 zucchini, spiralized into zucchini noodles (see tip)

2 cups kale

¾ cup shredded mint leaves

2 tbsp lemon juice

1 Heat 1 tablespoon of the olive oil in a large, heavy-based saucepan over medium heat. Cook the sliced green onions and the garlic, stirring, for 2 minutes or until softened.

2 Add the chicken; cook, stirring occasionally, for 2 minutes, or until the chicken has turned white on the outside. Add the potatoes, stock, and 1 cup water; bring to a boil. Reduce the heat to low and cook, covered, for 20 minutes, or until the potatoes are just tender and the chicken is cooked through.

3 Meanwhile, preheat a ridged cast-iron grill pan to high heat; grill the bread slices for 1 minute on each side or until toasted.

4 Remove the lid from the broth, and add the zucchini and kale. Cook, uncovered, for 1 minute until the kale is bright green. Remove the pan from the heat, then stir in three-quarters of the shredded mint and the lemon juice.

5 Divide the hot broth among 4 serving bowls. Thinly slice the reserved ends of the green onions; top the soup with the green onion and the remaining shredded mint. Drizzle each serving with a little of the remaining olive oil. Serve immediately with the toast.

TIP

If you don't have a spiralizer, you can shred the zucchini using a julienne peeler, mandoline, or V-slicer.

Salmon, fava bean, and labneh omelette

HIGH-PROTEIN | PREP + COOK TIME **20 MINUTES** | SERVES **4**

PER SERVING | Calories 568 | Carbohydrates 9g | Total sugars 4g | Fat 40g | Saturated fat 10g | Sodium 1.4g plus seasoning | Fiber 7g

Eggs, salmon, and broad beans combine here to make a high-protein, low-carb meal that is filling and tasty. Fava beans are rich in plant and soluble fiber, and also contain manganese—essential for good brain and nervous system function—folate, and other B vitamins. Instead of the labneh, you could use crumbled feta cheese or goat cheese, if you like.

8 eggs

1 lemon

1/3 cup extra virgin olive oil, divided

2 cups fava beans, blanched and peeled

1 cup fresh dill

4 green onions, thinly sliced

2/3 lb (300g) hot-smoked salmon, skin removed, flaked

5 oz (150g) labneh (see tip)

salt and freshly ground black pepper

lemon wedges, for serving

1 Lightly whisk the eggs with 2 tablespoons cold tap water in a large bowl until combined. Season with salt and pepper to taste.

2 Using a zesting tool, remove 1 tablespoon zest from the lemon (alternatively, finely grate the zest from the lemon). Squeeze the juice from the lemon; you will need 1 tablespoon of juice. Whisk together the lemon zest, lemon juice, and 2 tablespoons of the olive oil in a large bowl; season with salt and pepper to taste. Add the fava beans, dill, green onions, and salmon; toss gently to combine.

3 Heat 2 teaspoons of the olive oil in a 6 inch (15cm) nonstick skillet over medium heat. Add one-quarter of the egg mixture; using a spatula, pull the egg inward from the edge of the pan toward the center to create folds, letting the uncooked egg mixture fill any gaps. Cook for 2 minutes, or until done to your liking. Slide the omelette carefully onto a plate; fold over. Repeat three times with the remaining oil and the egg mixture to make a total of 4 omelettes.

4 Place the omelettes on 4 serving plates; top each one with some of the fava bean salad and labneh. Season with salt and pepper to taste. Serve with lemon wedges for squeezing over.

TIP

Labneh is a thick, creamy-textured yogurt with all its whey drained. To make your own, stir 1 teaspoon of sea salt flakes into 18oz (500g) of Greek yogurt. Spoon into a strainer lined with muslin or cheesecloth; place the strainer over a bowl, gather the cloth, and tie it tightly into a ball. Refrigerate for 24 hours until thick.

Indian scrambled eggs

HIGH-PROTEIN | PREP + COOK TIME **25 MINUTES** | SERVES **4**

PER SERVING | Calories 460 | Carbohydrates 37g | Total sugars 8g | Fat 24g | Saturated fat 9g | Sodium 1g plus seasoning | Fiber 5g

It's hard to eat poorly when you have a carton of eggs on hand, even if there's little else in the fridge or on the pantry shelves. Eggs represent compact packets of protein and nutrients ready to be turned into a nutritious meal in minutes.

½ cup shredded coconut

2 tbsp extra virgin olive oil, divided

2 long red chiles, thinly sliced

¼ cup ginger, peeled, shredded

½ cup red onion, thinly sliced

½ tsp garam masala

12 oz (400g) cherry tomatoes, halved

8 eggs

½ cup canned light coconut milk

2 limes

½ cup cilantro leaves

8 whole-grain flatbreads, warmed (see tip)

salt and freshly ground black pepper

1 Put the shredded coconut in a small heatsafe bowl; pour 1 cup boiling water over it. Set aside until needed.

2 Heat 1 tablespoon of the olive oil in a large nonstick frying pan over high heat. Add the chiles, ginger, red onion, and garam masala; cook, stirring, for 4 minutes, or until the onion softens. Next, add the tomatoes; cook, stirring occasionally, for 5 minutes longer until they soften and begin to burst. Transfer to a bowl; cover to keep warm. Wipe out the pan with a paper towel.

3 Meanwhile, whisk together the eggs and coconut milk until just combined. Season with salt and pepper to taste.

4 Heat the remaining olive oil in the cleaned pan over medium heat. Pour the egg mixture into the pan; cook, tilting the pan, until the egg mixture is almost set. Gently stir for 3 minutes, using a rubber spatula, or until the egg is just cooked.

5 Drain the soaked shredded coconut; return to the bowl. Finely grate the zest from 1 lime into the bowl; squeeze the juice from the lime (you will need 2 tablespoons of juice). Add the lime juice to the bowl; stir to combine. Cut the remaining lime into wedges.

6 Top the eggs with the warm tomato mixture, coconut mixture, and cilantro leaves. Serve with the warm flatbread and lime wedges for squeezing over.

TIP

Any type of flatbread will be delicious with this recipe, including the Lebanese handkerchief bread used here, Indian naan or rumali roti, or Greek pita bread.

Lentil, pear, and fennel salad with goat cheese

FAST | PREP + COOK TIME **30 MINUTES** | SERVES **4**

PER SERVING | Calories 677 | Carbohydrates 41g | Total sugars 18g | Fat 42g | Saturated fat 11g | Sodium 1.9g plus seasoning | Fiber 15g

Beans, lentils, and peas are packed with different types of fiber and a type of carbohydrate called resistant starch that is especially important for gut health. The friendly bacteria living in your colon thrive on resistant starch, and it is the product of this fermentation process that boosts our gut health and overall immune function.

1 cup French green lentils

⅓ cup extra virgin olive oil, divided

¼ cup flat-leaf parsley, coarsely chopped

2 Bosc pears, thinly sliced lengthwise (see tips)

1 cup walnuts, roasted

5 oz (150g) goat cheese, crumbled

¼ cup mint leaves

½ tsp dried chili flakes

salt and freshly ground black pepper

pickled fennel

1 large fennel bulb

1 tbsp sea salt flakes, divided

⅓ cup white wine vinegar

2 tsp sugar

1 Put the lentils and 3 cups cold tap water in a medium saucepan; bring to a boil. Reduce the heat to low; cook, partially covered with a lid, for 12 minutes or until the lentils are tender and the water has been absorbed. Remove from the heat. Add 1 tablespoon of the olive oil; season with salt and pepper to taste. Stir in the parsley; set aside.

2 To make the pickled fennel, trim the ends from the fennel, reserving 2 tablespoons of the fronds. Cut the fennel bulb in half lengthwise. Using a mandoline, V-slicer, or sharp knife, cut the fennel into very thin slices. Put in a colander with 2 teaspoons of the sea salt; let stand for 10 minutes. Rinse off the salt, then squeeze out any excess water. Transfer the fennel to a large bowl. Combine the remaining salt, vinegar, and sugar in a small bowl, stirring to dissolve the salt and sugar. Pour over the fennel; toss gently. Cover and refrigerate until needed.

3 Preheat a frying pan over high heat. Toss the pear slices with 1 tablespoon of the olive oil in a large bowl; season with a good grinding of pepper. Cook the pear slices for 3 minutes on each side or until browned.

4 Drain the pickled fennel, reserving the pickling liquid. To serve, layer the pear slices, lentils, and pickled fennel on a platter. Sprinkle with the walnuts, goat cheese, mint, chili flakes, and reserved fennel fronds. Drizzle with the reserved pickling liquid and remaining olive oil. Season with salt and pepper to taste.

TIPS

- Try Golden Delicious or Pink Lady apples instead of the pear, and pecan halves instead of walnuts.
- You can try other ingredients instead of goat cheese, including small fresh mozzarella balls or labneh, if you prefer.

Curry-roasted eggplant with dal salad

VEGETARIAN/HIGH-FIBER | PREP + COOK TIME **35 MINUTES** | SERVES **4**
PER SERVING | Calories 314 | Carbohydrates 17g | Total sugars 7g | Fat 20g | Saturated fat 6g | Sodium 0.49g plus seasoning | Fiber 9g

Packed with dietary fiber, eggplants are a good source of B vitamins, potassium, magnesium, and other minerals. Lentils up the fiber content of this dish, and also its essential nutrients quotient. If you can't find Chinese or Japanese eggplant, cut a large globe eggplant into thick wedges instead. You can also make the recipe with other curry pastes, such as korma.

6 Chinese or Japanese eggplants, halved lengthwise

2 tbsp tikka paste

2 tbsp extra virgin olive oil

1/2 cucumber

3/4 cup Greek yogurt

1 garlic clove, crushed

1 x 15 oz (425g) can brown lentils, drained, rinsed

2 cups pea shoots

2 tbsp lemon juice

salt and freshly ground black pepper

1/3 cup roasted unsalted cashews, chopped, to garnish

1 Preheat the oven to 400°F (200°C). Line a large baking sheet with parchment paper.

2 Using a sharp knife, score the cut sides of the eggplant in a crisscross pattern. Place the eggplant, cut-side up, on the prepared tray. Combine the tikka paste and olive oil; season with salt and pepper to taste. Spread over the cut side of the eggplant.

3 Roast the eggplant, cut-side up, for 15 minutes. Turn and cook for 10 minutes longer or until tender.

4 Meanwhile, coarsely grate the cucumber; squeeze out any excess liquid. Combine the cucumber, yogurt, and garlic in a small bowl. Season with salt and pepper to taste.

5 Combine the lentils, pea shoots, and lemon juice in a medium bowl. Season with salt and pepper to taste. Arrange the eggplant on a platter; spoon over the dal salad and cucumber-yogurt. Serve with the roasted cashews sprinkled over the top.

FILLING

Here you'll find plenty of filling and nutritious energy-boosting recipes to feed family and friends, from weeknight staples to healthier twists on comfort-food classics.

Baked carrot, haloumi cheese, and mint patties

FAST | PREP + COOK TIME **35 MINUTES** | SERVES **12**

PER SERVING | Calories 170 | Carbohydrates 12g | Total sugars 6g | Fat 9g | Saturated fat 3g | Sodium 0.8g plus seasoning | Fiber 4g

Beta-carotene is what makes carrots, sweet potato, and pumpkin orange. Beta-carotene can also be converted to vitamin A in the body. While diets rich in beta-carotene have been shown to benefit health, supplements do not have the same effect and can be harmful. Stick to real foods to gain all the benefits without any of the risks.

2 lb (1kg) carrots, coarsely grated

6 green onions, thinly sliced

6 oz (180g) haloumi cheese, coarsely grated

3 cups coarsely chopped mint leaves,
plus extra sprigs, to serve

$^2/_3$ cup whole-wheat flour

4 eggs, lightly beaten

extra virgin olive oil cooking spray

4 cups trimmed watercress sprigs

$^1/_2$ cup prepared baba ghanoush

salt and freshly ground black pepper

extra virgin olive oil for drizzling (optional)

1   Preheat the oven to 425°F (220°C). Line 2 baking sheets with parchment paper.

2   Put the carrots, green onions, haloumi cheese, mint leaves, flour, and eggs in a large bowl; stir to combine. Season with salt and pepper to taste.

3   Using a $^1/_2$-cup measure, divide the mixture into 12 portions. Place the portions 1$^1/_2$ inch (4cm) apart on the prepared trays; shape and flatten into 3 in (8cm) patties. Spray generously with the extra virgin olive oil.

4   Bake the patties for 30 minutes, swapping and rotating trays between shelves once during the cooking time.

5   Serve the baked patties with the watercress and extra mint sprigs; accompany it with the baba ghanoush, drizzled with extra virgin olive oil, if you like.

TIP

If you like , serve the patties stuffed into whole-wheat pita bread pockets or in very thin whole-grain flatbread.

Kidney bean, shrimp, and pepper fajita wraps

FAST | PREP + COOK TIME **20 MINUTES** | SERVES **4**

PER SERVING | Calories 448 | Carbohydrates 40g | Total sugars 12g | Fat 13g | Saturated fat 4g | Sodium 1.4g plus seasoning | Fiber 12g

Shrimp provides good levels of the long-chain omega-3 fats you might be taking as a fish oil supplement. These fats are crucially important when it comes to the brain and seem to play a role in cognitive function and brain health as we age.

1¼ lb (600g) medium uncooked shrimp, peeled and deveined, tails intact

2 tbsp extra virgin olive oil

1 tbsp chipotle hot sauce, plus extra ½ tsp

1 tsp smoked paprika

1 red onion, sliced into thin wedges

1 red bell pepper, seeded, sliced

1 yellow bell pepper, seeded, sliced

1 x 15½ oz (439g) can pinto beans, drained, rinsed

12 oz (400g) mixed cherry tomatoes, halved

4 x 8 in (20cm) whole-grain tortillas

½ cup light sour cream

salt and freshly ground black pepper

½ cup cilantro leaves, to garnish

1 Preheat a ridged cast-iron grill plate to a high heat.

2 Thread the shrimp onto 8 metal or soaked bamboo skewers; place on a tray. Put the olive oil, 1 tablespoon chipotle hot sauce, and paprika in a small bowl; mix well. Season with salt and pepper to taste. Brush 1½ tablespoons of the marinade over the shrimp skewers.

3 Heat the remaining marinade in a large skillet over high heat. Add the onion and sliced bell peppers; cook, stirring occasionally, for 4 minutes or until they start to turn golden and soften.

4 Add the pinto beans, tomatoes, and ¼ cup water to the pan; stir well. Cook for 4 minutes or until hot and the sauce thickens.

5 Meanwhile, grill the shrimp skewers for 1 minute on each side or until cooked through and grill marks appear. Grill the tortillas for 30 seconds on each side or until grill marks appear.

6 Divide the red and yellow pepper mixture among the tortillas; top each one with the grilled shrimp, sour cream, and a drizzle of the extra ½ teaspoon chipotle hot sauce. Serve the fajitas hot, sprinkled with the cilantro leaves.

Yogurt, kabocha squash, and pistachio pie

VEGETARIAN | PREP + COOK TIME **1 HOUR 20 MINUTES** | SERVES **4**

PER SERVING | Calories 510 | Carbohydrates 41g | Total sugars 8g | Fat 28g | Saturated fat 9g | Sodium 0.8g plus seasoning | Fiber 6g

Lutein and zeaxanthin are found in high concentrations in the eye and seem to play a crucial role in eye health. People with diets high in these two carotenoids reduce their risk of macular degeneration and developing cataracts. You'll find these nutrients in dark, leafy greens and Romaine lettuce, as well as in egg yolks.

1 lb (500g) kabocha squash, peeled, cut into ³/₄ in (2cm) pieces

1 tbsp extra virgin olive oil

¹/₃ cup pistachios

2 tbsp tahini

1¹/₄ cups Greek yogurt

2 eggs

2 tbsp fresh dill, divided

extra virgin olive oil cooking spray

6 sheets of fresh phyllo pastry (see tip)

¹/₄ tsp sumac

4 cups mixed green lettuce

salt and freshly ground black pepper

1 Preheat the oven to 350°F (180°C). Place the oven rack in the lowest position.

2 Put the squash and olive oil in a medium microwave-safe bowl; stir to coat the squash with the oil. Season with salt and pepper to taste. Cover with plastic wrap; microwave on high (100%), stirring halfway through, for 4 minutes 15 seconds or until just softened. Drain to remove any liquid; set aside to cool slightly.

3 In the bowl of a food processor, add the pistachios and tahini. Process until smooth. Add the yogurt, eggs, and 1 tablespoon of the dill; pulse until well combined. Transfer the yogurt mixture to a large bowl; stir in the cooled squash. Season with salt and pepper to taste.

4 Lightly spray a 9 inch (22cm) springform cake pan with the olive oil cooking spray. Place a sheet of phyllo over the top of the pan, then place a second sheet on top in the opposite direction; spray again with the oil. Repeat layering and spraying the remaining sheets of phyllo pastry. Gently press the layered pastry into the pan, letting the pastry edges overhang the top edge.

5 Pour the squash filling into the pastry case, and gently shake the pan to evenly distribute the pieces of squash. Fold in the excess pastry, scrunching it slightly to cover the filling. Spray with olive oil.

6 Bake the pie on the lowest rack for 1 hour or until the filling is just set and the pastry is golden. Remove from the pan immediately to prevent the pastry from steaming and becoming soggy. Top the pie with the remaining dill; dust with the sumac. Serve with the lettuce.

TIPS

- If you like, you can swap sweet potatoes for the squash, and almonds for the pistachios.
- Fresh phyllo pastry from the refrigerated section of the supermarket is less brittle than frozen phyllo, and therefore less likely to tear as you work with it. If you cannot find chilled phyllo pastry, use thawed frozen phyllo instead.

Salmon and olive salsa verde with fennel and Swiss chard salad

HEALTHY FATS | PREP **25 MINUTES** | SERVES **4**

PER SERVING | Calories 822 | Carbohydrates 26g | Total sugars 9g | Fat 57g | Saturated fat 9g | Sodium 1.9g plus seasoning | Fiber 13g

People in cultures where a lot of fish and seafood is traditionally eaten have lower levels of depression. There is ongoing research into this area, but evidence certainly suggests that upping the intake of omega-3s, which are found in salmon, can help reduce depressive symptoms in some people.

2½ tbsp extra virgin olive oil, divided

1 sweet potato, skin on, thinly sliced lengthwise

4 x ½lb (250g) salmon fillets, skin on

1 large fennel bulb, thinly sliced

4 Swiss chard leaves, finely shredded

sea salt and freshly ground black pepper

green olive salsa verde

¾ cup pitted Sicilian green olives

1 tbsp baby capers

1 garlic clove

3 cups flat-leaf parsley

1 tbsp red wine vinegar

⅓ cup extra virgin olive oil

1 Heat 2 tablespoons of the olive oil in a large nonstick pan over high heat. Cook the sweet potato, in batches, for 1 minute on each side or until golden and cooked through. Transfer to a baking sheet lined with paper towels; season with salt and pepper to taste.

2 Heat the remaining olive oil in the same pan over high heat. Sprinkle the salmon skin with sea salt and a good grinding of pepper. Cook the salmon, skin-side down, for 4 minutes or until the skin is crisp. Turn; cook for 2 more minutes or until the salmon is just cooked through.

3 Meanwhile, to make the green olive salsa verde, put the olives, capers, garlic, and parsley in the bowl of a food processor. Process until finely chopped. Add the vinegar, olive oil, and ⅓ cup water; process until well combined.

4 Put the fennel, Swiss chard, and ½ cup of the green olive salsa verde in a large bowl; toss to mix through.

5 Divide the salmon, sweet potato, and fennel salad among 4 serving plates. Serve with the remaining salsa verde.

Ricotta, asparagus, fava bean, and mint risotto

HIGH-FIBER | PREP + COOK TIME **55 MINUTES** | SERVES **4**

PER SERVING | Calories 536 | Carbohydrates 65g | Total sugars 6g | Fat 20g | Saturated fat 6g | Sodium 0.2g | Fiber 10g

Brown rice retains the bran and germ, which are removed during the milling process for white rice. Both types of rice are high in carbohydrates; however, the whole-grain nature of brown rice means it has more fiber, vitamins, and minerals than its white counterpart.

³/₄ lb (340g) fresh asparagus, trimmed

4 cups vegetable stock

¹/₄ cup extra virgin olive oil, divided

¹/₂ cup finely chopped onion

2 garlic cloves, crushed

1¹/₂ cups uncooked brown rice

1 cup mint leaves, divided

³/₄ cup ricotta cheese

1¹/₂ cups fava beans, peeled (thawed if frozen)

1 large lemon

¹/₃ cup finely grated Parmesan cheese

freshly ground black pepper

1 Cut the asparagus spears into 4 inch (10cm) lengths; halve or quarter lengthwise depending on the thickness. Thinly slice the remaining bottom half of the asparagus into rounds.

2 Pour the vegetable stock and 1¹/₂ cups water into a medium saucepan; bring to a boil over high heat. Reduce the heat to low.

3 Meanwhile, heat a large sauté pan over medium heat. Add 2 tablespoons of the olive oil. Cook the onion and garlic, stirring frequently, for 2 minutes or until softened. Add the rice; stir to coat the grains in the mixture.

4 Add three-quarters of the hot stock mixture to the pan; remove the remaining stock (still in the pan) from the heat. Cook the risotto, covered, over low heat for 35 minutes, or until the liquid has been absorbed and the rice is tender. Stir the rice a few times during the cooking time to prevent it from sticking to the bottom of the pan.

5 Meanwhile, add the asparagus spears to the remaining stock; bring back to a boil. Simmer for 1 minute until just tender. Remove from the heat. Using a pair of tongs, transfer the asparagus to a plate. Reserve stock.

6 Reserve 2 tablespoons of the small mint leaves for serving later. In a bowl, mix the remaining mint and the ricotta cheese until smooth.

7 Uncover the rice; increase the heat to high. Stir in the remaining stock, asparagus, and fava beans. Cook, stirring frequently, for 10 minutes or until thickened.

8 Grate 2 teaspoons zest from the lemon; squeeze the juice from the lemon (you will need 2 teaspoons). Add the ricotta mixture, Parmesan cheese, lemon zest, and juice to the risotto; stir to combine. Season with pepper. Top with the asparagus spears, reserved mint leaves, and remaining olive oil.

TIPS

- Customize the vegetables to your taste and to the season. Try broccolini instead of asparagus, and peas in place of fava beans.
- Make this recipe vegetarian by using a vegetarian hard cheese instead of Parmesan cheese.

One-pan pork and almond meatballs with kale and broccolini

HIGH-PROTEIN | PREP **25 MINUTES** | SERVES **4**

PER SERVING | Calories 477 | Carbohydrates 8g | Total sugars 7g | Fat 31g | Saturated fat 7g | Sodium 0.7g plus seasoning | Fiber 4g

Kale is one of the most nutritious leafy greens. It's particularly rich in carotenoids, which can be converted to vitamin A in the body. A single cup of kale provides you with more than 200 percent of the daily recommended amount of vitamin A.

$\frac{1}{2}$ cup blanched almonds, roasted, finely chopped, plus extra, to garnish

1 lb (450g) ground pork

2 garlic cloves, crushed

1 egg

$\frac{1}{4}$ cup finely chopped tarragon, plus extra 3 sprigs

2 tsp finely grated lemon zest

$\frac{1}{3}$ cup finely grated Parmesan cheese, plus extra, to garnish

2 tsp extra virgin olive oil

$2\frac{1}{2}$ cups almond milk

1 tbsp Dijon mustard

6 oz (175g) broccolini, blanched, trimmed, halved lengthwise (see tip)

$\frac{1}{2}$ lb (250g) kale, trimmed, chopped

salt and freshly ground black pepper

1 In a large bowl, combine the pork, almonds, garlic, egg, tarragon, lemon zest, and $\frac{1}{3}$ cup Parmesan cheese in a large bowl; season with salt and pepper to taste. Roll into tablespoon-sized balls.

2 In a large, deep-sided sauté pan, heat the olive oil over medium heat. Add the meatballs and cook on each side, turning, for 4 minutes or until browned.

3 Add the almond milk, extra 3 sprigs of tarragon, and Dijon mustard; bring to a simmer. Cook for 6 minutes or until the mixture has reduced slightly; season with salt and pepper to taste.

4 Add the broccolini and kale; gently toss. Cook for 2 minutes; season with salt and pepper to taste. Serve with the extra almonds and Parmesan cheese sprinkled over the top.

TIP

To blanch the broccolini, place it in a heatproof bowl; cover with boiling water. Let stand for 2 minutes; drain.

Donburi with mushrooms and salmon

HIGH-PROTEIN | PREP + COOK TIME **35 MINUTES** | SERVES **12**

PER SERVING | Calories 555 | Carbohydrates 39g | Total sugars 6g | Fat 29g | Saturated fat 5g | Sodium 2.8g | Fiber 4.5g

The Japanese dish donburi is named after its cooking style and the oversized rice bowl in which it's served. Ingredients vary, from fish and meat to vegetables, but they are always simmered in a sauce and served over rice. Mushrooms provide B vitamins and essential minerals; ginger and garlic both contain powerful antioxidants.

3 cups brown rice and quinoa, cooked or prepared per package instructions

2 tbsp extra virgin olive oil, divided

³/₄ lb (300g) mixed wild mushrooms, such as oyster, shiitake, and enoki, large mushrooms halved

4 green onions, thinly sliced

1 tbsp fresh ginger, grated

2 garlic cloves, crushed

1 long red chile, seeded, finely chopped

¹/₄ cup light soy sauce

2 tbsp sake

1 tbsp mirin

4 x 4 oz (120g) salmon fillets, skin on

sliced long red chile, to garnish

sliced green onion, to garnish

lime wedges, for serving

1   Heat 1 tablespoon of the olive oil in a wok over high heat; stir-fry the mushrooms for 3 minutes or until lightly golden. Add the green onions, ginger, garlic, and finely chopped chile; stir-fry for 1 minute longer until fragrant. Combine the soy sauce, sake, and mirin in a bowl; add the rice-quinoa mixture. Add this to the mushrooms; stir-fry until combined.

2   Meanwhile, heat the remaining olive oil in a large skillet over high heat; cook the salmon fillets, skin-side down, for 3 minutes or until the skin is crisp. Turn and cook for 2 more minutes for medium rare, or until the salmon is cooked to your liking.

3   Divide the rice mixture in 4 serving bowls; top with the salmon. Serve topped with the extra sliced chile and green onion, with lime wedges for squeezing over.

Eggplant and zucchini yogurt casserole

VEGETARIAN | PREP + COOK TIME **1 HOUR 15 MINUTES** | SERVES **4**

PER SERVING | Calories 658 | Carbohydrates 31g | Total sugars 21g | Fat 45g | Saturated fat 21g | Sodium 1.3g plus seasoning | Fiber 8g

Tomatoes contain the carotenoid lycopene, an antioxidant that gives them their red color and may be useful in reducing the risk of some cancers and heart disease. While cooking does slightly reduce the vitamin C content in tomatoes, it actually increases the lycopene content.

1¼ lb (600g) globe eggplant, cut into ½ in (1.3cm) pieces

½ cup thinly sliced onion

¼ cup extra virgin olive oil, divided

1 tbsp cumin seeds

½ lb (260g) vine-ripened tomatoes

½ lb (240g) zucchini, cut into ½ in (1.3cm) pieces

1 x 14½ oz (411g) can crushed tomatoes

¼ cup oregano leaves, finely chopped, divided

¼ cup rice flour

3 cups Greek yogurt

3 eggs

4 oz (120g) marinated feta cheese, drained

salt and freshly ground black pepper

1 Preheat the oven to 425°F (220°C). Preheat a large baking sheet in the oven for 5 minutes.

2 In a large bowl, toss the eggplant, onion, and cumin seeds with 1 tbsp of the olive oil. Season well with salt and pepper. Spread the vegetables on the preheated baking sheet. Arrange the vine tomatoes on top; roast the vegetables for 10 minutes.

3 Remove the vine tomatoes, and set aside for serving. Add the zucchini, canned tomatoes, and half of the oregano to the tray with the vegetables; stir to mix. Roast for 15 more minutes or until golden.

4 Spoon the eggplant mixture into four 6 inch (16cm) (1½ cups/375ml) round oven-safe dishes. Set aside.

5 Heat the remaining olive oil in a medium saucepan over medium heat. Add the rice flour and whisk for 2 minutes, or until the mixture is pale and frothy. Remove the pan from the heat; whisk in the yogurt and eggs until combined.

6 Spoon the yogurt mixture over the vegetables in the dishes, dividing it among them evenly; sprinkle with feta cheese. Bake for 18 minutes or until golden and bubbling. Serve topped with the roasted vine tomatoes and the remaining oregano leaves.

TIP

For an approach that's lower in fat, use a 50:50 mix of ricotta cheese and Greek yogurt (or a non-dairy yogurt alternative).

Korean-style shrimp pancakes

HIGH-PROTEIN | PREP + COOK TIME **40 MINUTES** | SERVES **4**
PER SERVING | Calories 825 | Carbohydrates 73g | Total sugars 8g | Fat 28g | Saturated fat 5g | Sodium 2.3g plus seasoning | Fiber 10g

Green onion pancakes, or *pajeon*, are a Korean favorite. Usually made with a mixture of wheat and rice flours, they are large fritter-like pancakes chock-full of fresh ingredients. For a vegetarian version of the pancakes, use a flavored tofu or tempeh, cut into cubes or batons.

2 cups whole-wheat flour

1/3 cup brown rice flour

4 eggs

2 tbsp sesame seeds, toasted, divided

1/3 cup coconut aminos

1 tbsp palm sugar

2 tbsp lime juice

1/4 cup extra virgin olive oil , divided

2 lb (1kg) uncooked shrimp, peeled and deveined, halved lengthwise

8 green onions, trimmed, quartered lengthwise

1/3 cup cilantro, finely chopped, plus extra for serving (optional)

salt and freshly ground black pepper

1 In a large bowl, whisk together the flours, 2 1/2 cups ice-cold water, eggs, and 1 tablespoon of the sesame seeds until just combined; season with salt and pepper to taste. Refrigerate the batter for 10 minutes.

2 Meanwhile, put the coconut aminos, palm sugar, and lime juice in a screw-top jar with a tight-fitting lid; shake well to combine. Set aside until needed.

3 Heat 1 tablespoon of the olive oil in an 8 inch (23cm) oven-safe nonstick frying pan over high heat; cook the shrimp, in batches, for 1 minute or until just cooked through and lightly golden. Transfer to a bowl. Reserve the pan.

4 Meanwhile, preheat the oven to 425°F (220°C).

5 In the pan the shrimp was cooked in, heat 2 teaspoons of the olive oil over medium heat; pour in one-quarter of the batter; top with one-quarter each of the green onions, cooked shrimp, and cilantro. Cook, covered, for 3 minutes or until the bottom is set.

6 Transfer the pancake (still in the pan) to the oven; cook for 1 minute longer or until lightly golden and cooked through. Slide the pancake onto a plate; cover to keep warm. Repeat with the remaining ingredients to make a total of 4 pancakes.

7 Drizzle the pancakes with the dressing; sprinkle with the remaining sesame seeds. Serve topped with extra cilantro leaves, if you like.

TIPS

• Instead serve the pancakes topped with curled green onion tops and micro herbs, if you like.
• This recipe is also delicious with kecap manis, a distinctively flavored Indonesian sweet soy sauce with a syrupy consistency. Use it instead of the coconut aminos and palm sugar in the dressing.

Broccolini pasta with gooey eggs

VEGETARIAN | PREP + COOK TIME **30 MINUTES** | SERVES **4**

PER SERVING | Calories 508 | Carbohydrates 38g | Total sugars 4g | Fat 26g | Saturate fat 5g | Sodium 0.4g plus seasoning | Fiber 8g

Brief cooking is the best way to preserve the nutrients in green vegetables like broccolini and other brassicas. You can also throw them into dishes in the last moments of cooking until just softened. If you cook them for too long, they will not taste very nice, and they'll also lose their bright green color.

8 oz (227g) dried buckwheat pasta

6 eggs, room temperature

2 tbsp extra virgin olive oil

$1/2$ cup finely chopped walnuts

2 garlic cloves, thinly sliced

1 long red chile, seeded, finely chopped

$3/4$ lb (350g) broccolini, trimmed, halved lengthwise

1 large lemon

salt and freshly ground black pepper

1 Fill a large bowl with ice cubes and water. Place near the burner.

2 Bring a large saucepan of salted water to a boil. Add the buckwheat pasta, return to a boil, and cook for 2 minutes. Carefully add the eggs and cook with the pasta, keeping at a boil, for 6 more minutes. Using a slotted spoon, transfer the soft-boiled eggs to the ice water.

3 Add the broccolini to the saucepan with the pasta; cook for 1 minute or until the pasta and broccolini are both just tender. Drain the pasta and broccolini, reserving $1/2$ cup of the cooking water.

4 Meanwhile, heat the olive oil in a large pan over medium-low heat; cook the walnuts, garlic, and chile, stirring, for 3 minutes or until the garlic and walnuts are lightly golden. Season with salt and pepper to taste.

5 Grate 2 teaspoons zest from the lemon, then squeeze the juice from it (you will need $1/4$ cup of lemon juice). Add the pasta and broccolini to the walnut mixture with the lemon zest and juice. Season with salt and pepper to taste; toss well.

6 Divide the pasta among 4 serving bowls. Peel the eggs; break open over each bowl of pasta, allowing the soft yolks to disperse as a sauce.

Beans and tofu with crispy pitas

HIGH-PROTEIN | PREP + COOK TIME **35 MINUTES** | SERVES **4**

PER SERVING | Calories 895 | Carbohydrates 114g | Total sugars 28g | Fat 26g | Saturated fat 4g | Sodium 2.9g plus seasoning | Fiber 24g

Chickpeas are a great source of protein, complex carbohydrates, minerals, and several vitamins. Serving the chickpeas with whole-grain pita bread also means you get the full spectrum of essential amino acids.

1/3 cup extra virgin olive oil, divided

8 oz (225g) firm tofu, coarsely crumbled

1/2 tsp chili flakes

1 cup firmly packed flat-leaf parsley, half coarsely chopped

1 cup thinly sliced red onion

3/4 cup coarsely grated carrots

1 x 28 oz (794g) can crushed tomatoes

1 x 15 1/2 oz (439g) can chickpeas, drained, rinsed

1 x 15 oz (425g) can black beans, drained, rinsed

2 tbsp Worcestershire sauce

2 tbsp Dijon mustard

2 tbsp pure maple syrup

4 whole-grain pita pocket breads

salt and freshly ground black pepper

1 Heat 2 tablespoons of the olive oil in a large frying pan over medium heat; cook the tofu, turning frequently, for 6 minutes or until golden. Add the chili and chopped parsley; cook for 30 seconds. Transfer with a slotted spoon to a plate lined with paper towels. Set aside to keep warm.

2 Return the pan to the heat. Add 1 tablespoon of the olive oil; cook the onion for 5 minutes or until starting to brown.

3 Add the carrots, tomatoes, chickpeas, black beans, Worcestershire sauce, Dijon mustard, and maple syrup to the pan; cook, stirring occasionally, for 20 minutes or until the mixture is thickened. Season with salt and pepper to taste.

4 Meanwhile, preheat the oven to 425°F (220°C). Place a wire cooling rack over a large baking sheet. Split the pita breads in half; place each one on the rack, open with the crust side down. Brush with the remaining oil. Bake in 2 batches, cut-side up, for 4 minutes or until golden. Remove and keep warm.

5 Serve the crispy pita breads topped with the bean mixture, crisp tofu, and remaining parsley leaves.

TIP

You can swap the black beans for kidney beans instead, if you like.

Veggie patch pies

HIGH-FIBER | PREP + COOK TIME **1 HOUR 15 MINUTES** | SERVES **4**

PER SERVING | Calories 784 | Carbohydrates 85g | Total sugars 21g | Fat 33g | Saturated fat 5g | Sodium 1.8g plus seasoning | Fiber 19g

This recipe has it all: a good array of vegetables and protein, and fiber from the beans and oats. As a bonus, the walnuts offer a veritable array of antioxidant and anti-inflammatory nutrients, as well as valuable monounsaturated and hard-to-source omega-3 fatty acids.

1 lb (500g) sweet potatoes, peeled

5 large portabello caps

³/₄ lb (300g) globe eggplant

2 tbsp extra virgin olive oil

1 tsp ground cumin

1 tsp paprika

1 x 15 oz (425g) can black beans, drained, rinsed

1 x 15¹/₂ oz (439g) can red kidney beans, drained, rinsed

2 cups tomato pasta sauce

salt and freshly ground black pepper

pie topping

1 whole-grain pita pocket bread

¹/₂ cup rolled (old-fashioned) oats, divided

¹/₂ cup walnuts, divided

¹/₄ cup extra virgin olive oil

¹/₃ cup finely grated Parmesan cheese

1 tbsp thyme leaves, plus extra for serving

1   Preheat the oven to 425°F (220°C). Line 2 large baking sheets with parchment paper.

2   Cut the potato into 1 inch (2.5cm) pieces. Cut the mushrooms and eggplant into ³/₄ inch (2cm) pieces. In a large bowl, toss the vegetables with the oil and spices; season well with salt and a good grinding of pepper. Arrange on the baking sheets in a single layer. Roast for 30 minutes or until the vegetables are soft and golden brown, swapping the trays between shelves halfway through the cooking time.

3   Meanwhile, to make the pie topping, coarsely tear the pita bread. In the bowl of a food processor, add the pita bread, ¹/₄ cup rolled oats, ¹/₄ cup walnuts, and the olive oil. Pulse until chopped and combined. In a bowl, mix the chopped mixture with the Parmesan cheese, the thyme, and remaining oats and walnuts.

4   In a separate bowl, combine the black beans, red kidney beans, and pasta sauce. Stir in the hot cooked vegetables; season with salt and pepper to taste. Divide the mixture evenly among four 2-cup oven-safe dishes. Divide the topping among the dishes.

5   Bake the pies for 20 minutes or until the tops are golden and the filling is bubbling. Serve topped with the remaining thyme leaves.

Cauliflower "butter chicken"

VEGETARIAN | PREP + COOK TIME **40 MINUTES** | SERVES **4**

PER SERVING | Calories 436 | Carbohydrates 30g | Total sugars 19g | Fat 26g | Saturated fat 6g | Sodium 0.2g plus seasoning | Fiber 10g

Cauliflower replaces chicken in this vegetarian take on butter chicken. Numerous studies have shown that veggies like cauliflower offer some protection against cancers, heart disease, and the functional declines associated with aging. Serve this dish with steamed rice.

3¼ lb (1.5kg) cauliflower

¼ cup extra virgin olive oil, divided

½ cup finely chopped onion

2 garlic cloves, crushed

1 tbsp fresh ginger, grated

¼ cup finely chopped cilantro, plus extra to serve

1 tsp garam masala

1 tsp ground cumin

1 tsp smoked paprika

1 cinnamon stick

1½ cups tomato sauce

4 tbsp tomato paste

1 cup vegetable stock

½ cup Greek yogurt

½ cup unsalted roasted cashews

salt and freshly ground black pepper

steamed rice, for serving

1 Cut the cauliflower into medium-sized florets. Heat 2 tablespoons of the olive oil in a large, deep frying pan over medium heat; cook the cauliflower, in 2 batches and turning occasionally, for 10 minutes or until dark golden and cooked through. Remove the cauliflower from the pan; wipe the pan clean.

2 Heat the remaining olive oil in the same pan over medium heat; cook the onion for 5 minutes or until softened. Add the garlic, ginger, cilantro, and spices; cook for 30 seconds or until fragrant.

3 Add the tomato sauce, tomato paste, and vegetable stock; bring to a simmer and cook, covered, for 10 minutes. Stir in the yogurt. Season with salt and pepper to taste. Add the cauliflower to the sauce; cook for 5 minutes or until warmed through.

4 Sprinkle the cauliflower with the cashews and extra cilantro leaves.

Golden cauliflower gnocchi with Swiss chard

VEGETARIAN/LOW-CARB | PREP + COOK TIME **50 MINUTES** | SERVES **4**

PER SERVING | Calories 534 | Carbohydrates 59g | Total sugars 19g | Fat 24g | Saturated fat 3g | Sodium 1g plus seasoning | Fiber 8g

Cauliflower is a versatile vegetable, making it a great low-carb alternative for typically high-carb ingredients such as rice and dishes such as gnocchi. In the recipe here, it replaces potatoes and white flour for a delicious gnocchi with Swiss chard and hazelnuts.

2 lb (1 kg) cauliflower, cut into 1¼ in (3cm) florets (see tip)

1½ cups white spelt flour, plus extra, to dust

¼ tsp ground nutmeg

⅓ cup extra virgin olive oil, plus extra for greasing

1½ lb (700g) Swiss chard, stems thinly sliced, leaves torn

2 tsp finely grated lemon zest

2 tbsp lemon juice

⅓ cup coarsely chopped toasted hazelnuts, to garnish

½ tsp dried chili flakes, to garnish

salt and freshly ground black pepper

1 Steam the cauliflower in a covered steamer basket, over a saucepan of boiling water, for 8 minutes or until tender. Transfer the cauliflower to a clean dish towel or cheesecloth; allow to cool for 5 minutes. Squeeze out as much excess liquid as possible, until the cauliflower feels dry.

2 Process the cauliflower with the spelt flour, nutmeg, and salt and pepper to taste until the mixture just comes together as a ball of dough. Turn out the dough onto a lightly floured work surface; knead gently until smooth. Cut the dough into 4 equal portions. Cover with a clean dish towel.

3 Roll each dough portion into a ¾ inch (2cm) thick rope, about 11½ inches (29cm) long. Cut into ¾ inch (2cm) pieces. Transfer to a lightly floured tray.

4 Cook the gnocchi, in batches, in a large saucepan of boiling salted water for 3 minutes or until the gnocchi float to the surface. Remove the gnocchi from the pan with a slotted spoon. Transfer to an oiled baking sheet. Reserve ½ cup of the cooking water.

5 Heat 2 tablespoons of the olive oil in large, deep frying pan over medium heat. Cook the gnocchi, tossing, for 3 minutes or until golden brown. Remove from the pan; set aside to keep warm. Heat the remaining oil in the same pan over medium heat. Cook the chard stems for 3 minutes or until almost soft. Add the chard leaves and reserved cooking water. Cook, stirring, for 1 minute until just wilted. Stir in the lemon zest and juice. Season well with salt and a good grinding of pepper, and remove the pan from the heat.

6 Divide the chard mixture among 4 serving bowls. Top with the gnocchi, and sprinkle with the chopped hazelnuts and chili flakes to serve.

TIP

Once you have trimmed the cauliflower, weigh it, as you will need 1¾ lb (850g) to make the gnocchi.

Sides

Each of these side dishes is more than an afterthought for expanding a meal into something more substantial—and more than just a quick way to get more vegetables onto a plate. Filled with vibrant, health-boosting ingredients, they will tempt even the fussiest eater.

Sweet potato and chickpea mash

PREP + COOK TIME **30 MINUTES** | SERVES **4**

Peel and coarsely chop 2 lb (1 kg) sweet potatoes. Put them in a medium saucepan with enough cold water to just cover. Boil over medium heat for 15 minutes or until the sweet potatoes are tender; drain. During the last 5 minutes of cooking time, add a drained and rinsed 15 oz (425g) can chickpeas. Return the sweet potato mixture to the pan; mash until smooth (or use a potato ricer). Add 2 tablespoons garlic-infused olive oil, 1 tablespoon tahini, and 1 tablespoon lemon juice; fold in gently until the mash is smooth. Season with salt and freshly ground black pepper to taste.

Broccoli and cauliflower rice

PREP + COOK TIME **15 MINUTES** | SERVES **4**

Trim the ends off 1½ lb (700g) fresh broccoli; discard. Cut the broccoli into florets. Remove the outside leaves, base, and any tough, thick stalks from 1½ lb (700g) cauliflower; discard. Cut the cauliflower into florets. Using a food processor, pulse the florets, in small batches, with ¼ teaspoon sea salt flakes until the consistency of rice. Working in batches, place the vegetable "rice" in the center of a clean cheesecloth. Gather the ends of the cloth together to enclose the rice, then twist, squeezing tightly, to remove as much excess moisture as possible. The broccoli and cauliflower rice can be eaten raw in salads or stir-fried like rice.

Garlicky green beans and peas with pine nuts

PREP + COOK TIME **15 MINUTES** | SERVES **4**

Trim ½ lb (225g) each of baby green beans, sugar snap peas, and snow peas. Set aside. Stir 2 thinly sliced garlic cloves, ¼ cup olive oil, and 2 tablespoons pine nuts in a nonstick frying pan over medium heat for 4 minutes or until garlic is golden. Strain into a bowl; reserve the oil. Whisk 1 tablespoon lemon juice and 2 teaspoons Dijon mustard into the reserved oil. Boil a large saucepan of salted water. Cook beans 1 minute; then add sugar snap peas; cook 1 more minute. Add snow peas; cook 1 minute longer. Drain; cool under cold water. Toss greens with dressing. Sprinkle with garlic and pine nuts. Season with salt and freshly ground black pepper.

Corn on the cob with Parmesan cheese

PREP + COOK TIME **15 MINUTES** | SERVES **4**

Boil 6 ears of corn with the husks on for 15 minutes. Drain; cool in the husks. Peel back husks, discarding silks. Tie the husks back with kitchen string. Heat ¼ cup olive oil in small saucepan. Add 1 crushed garlic clove, 2 tablespoons coarsely chopped pine nuts, 1 teaspoon salt, and ¼ teaspoon freshly ground black pepper; cook for 2 minutes or until nuts are golden. Brush the cobs with the oil mixture, then roll in ¾ cup finely grated Parmesan cheese combined with ¼ cup finely chopped flat-leaf parsley.

Moroccan lamb pilaf

HIGH-PROTEIN/FAST | PREP + COOK TIME **30 MINUTES** | SERVES **4**

PER SERVING | Calories 568 | Carbohydrates 64g | Total sugars 9g | Fat 20g | Saturated fat 6g | Sodium 0.4g | Fiber 11g

Bulgur is whole-grain wheat parboiled and cracked into different grades of fineness. Whole grains contain all three parts of the grain kernel: the bran, germ, and endosperm. There is strong evidence that eating whole grains is good for us, reducing our risk of chronic diseases.

2 tbsp extra virgin olive oil

¾ cup thinly sliced onion

½ lb (225g) ground lamb

2 tbsp harissa seasoning, plus extra, for serving (optional)

½ bunch of cilantro, finely chopped, plus extra, to garnish

1½ cups coarse bulgur wheat, rinsed well

1 x 15 oz (425g) can chickpeas, drained, rinsed

1 cup julienned carrots

¼ cup natural sliced almonds, toasted, to garnish

⅓ cup Greek yogurt, for serving

salt and freshly ground pepper

1 Heat the olive oil in a large, heavy-based saucepan over medium-high heat; cook the onion for 8 minutes or until golden brown and slightly crispy. Increase the heat to high; cook the lamb, breaking up any lumps with a wooden spoon, for 5 minutes or until well browned.

2 Add the harissa seasoning and cilantro; cook, stirring, for 1 minute or until fragrant. Add the bulgur wheat; cook, stirring, for 1 minute or until toasted. Add the chickpeas and 1½ cups water; bring to a boil. Reduce the heat to low; cook, covered, for 15 minutes or until the liquid has been absorbed. Remove from the heat; let stand, covered, for 5 minutes. Season with salt and pepper to taste.

3 Fluff up the bulgur grains with a fork. Top the pilaf with the carrots, reserved cilantro leaves, and almonds. Serve with the yogurt, dusted with extra harissa seasoning, if you like.

Harissa fish sticks with mashed potatoes and peas

HIGH-PROTEIN | PREP + COOK TIME **35 MINUTES** | SERVES **4**

PER SERVING | Calories 905 | Carbohydrates 57g | Total sugars 8g | Fat 49g | Saturated fat 13g | Sodium 0.9g plus seasoning | Fiber 10g

We've given classic fish sticks a healthier makeover using salmon and whole-grain bread crumbs, and replaced traditional tartar sauce with a tangy yogurt harissa sauce for spooning over or serving alongside the fish sticks.

extra virgin olive oil cooking spray

1¼ lb (600g) russet potatoes, peeled, chopped

2½ cups frozen peas

¼ cup extra virgin olive oil

½ cup mint, coarsely chopped, plus extra sprigs, for serving

1½ lb (700g) skinless salmon fillets

1¼ cups Greek yogurt

1½ tbsp harissa paste

1 tbsp cornichons, drained, finely chopped

1 tbsp capers, finely chopped

4 slices of stale whole-grain bread, torn into chunks

salt and freshly ground black pepper

lemon wedges, for serving

1 Preheat the oven to 425°F (220°C). Place a wire cooling rack over a large baking sheet. Spray the rack with olive oil cooking spray.

2 Put the potatoes in a medium saucepan of cold water over high heat. Bring to a boil; cook for 20 minutes, adding the peas during the last 1 minute of cooking time. Drain; let the vegetables stand in the colander for 2 minutes to drain well. Return to the saucepan. Using a potato masher, crush the potato and peas with the olive oil and mint. Season with salt and pepper to taste; cover to keep warm.

3 Cut the fish into 16 even finger-shaped pieces, each about 1¼ x 4¾ inches (3cm x 12cm). Carefully place the fish sticks in a large bowl, taking care not to break them into pieces.

4 Combine the yogurt and harissa in a medium bowl; season with salt and pepper to taste. Add a heaping ⅓ cup of the yogurt mixture to the fish; toss to coat evenly. Stir the cornichons and capers into the remaining yogurt mixture; refrigerate the sauce until needed.

5 In the bowl of a food processor, add the stale bread; pulse to form coarse bread crumbs. Sprinkle the crumbs evenly over the fish; press down on the crumbs to secure them to the fish. (Because the crumbs are chunky, they may not completely coat the fish.) Arrange the fish fingers on the prepared rack in a single layer, pressing any uncoated areas with the bread crumbs. Spray the fish sticks generously with olive oil.

6 Bake the fish sticks for 12 minutes or until the crumbs are golden and crisp and the fish is cooked through, flipping once while cooking. Serve immediately with the mashed potatoes and peas, harissa yogurt sauce, extra mint sprigs, and lemon wedges for squeezing over.

TIP

You can use a firm white fish in place of salmon if you prefer. You can also use canned salmon. Simply drain any juices from the fish before using.

Stovetop green chile eggs with paneer

VEGETARIAN | PREP + COOK TIME **45 MINUTES** | SERVES **4**

PER SERVING | Calories 676 | Carbohydrates 43g | Total sugars 5g | Fat 37g | Saturated fat 13g | Sodium 0.8g plus seasoning | Fiber 5g

A serving of two large eggs provides 580 calories, 12.7g of protein, 10.3g of fat, and 1.4g of carbohydrates. Of the fat, less than a third is saturated fat and more than half is healthy monounsaturated fat—the same family of fats found in olive oil and avocados.

1³/₄ lb (800g) waxy new potatoes, cut into ¹/₂ in (1cm) slices

2¹/₂ tbsp extra virgin olive oil, divided

2 tbsp curry leaves, divided

³/₄ cup thinly sliced onion

2 long green chiles, seeded, finely chopped

¹/₂ cup cilantro, finely chopped

2 tsp garam masala

1 tsp cumin seeds

¹/₂ tsp ground turmeric

12 eggs, divided

2 cups spinach leaves

8 oz (225g) paneer, crumbled

salt and freshly ground black pepper

1 Bring a large saucepan of water to a boil; add the sliced potatoes and cook for 8 minutes or until just tender. (Do not overcook the potatoes or they will break up during the second cooking in the frying pan, later.) Drain well.

2 Heat 2 tablespoons of the olive oil in a 10 inch (25cm) frying pan over high heat. Add the curry leaves; cook for 1 minute or until crisp. Remove; drain on paper towels. Cook the onion in the same pan for 4 minutes or until softened. Add the chiles, cilantro, and spices; cook for 30 seconds longer. Remove from the pan.

3 Whisk 8 of the eggs in a large bowl. Arrange the sliced potatoes in the pan. Top with the onion mixture, half of the curry leaves, and the spinach. Pour in the beaten egg. Season with salt and pepper to taste. Make 4 indentations in the top of the egg mixture; crack the remaining eggs into each hole, and sprinkle with the paneer. Season with salt and pepper to taste.

4 Cover the frying pan with a tight-fitting lid. Cook over low heat for 20 minutes or until the eggs are set and cooked to your liking. Serve immediately, topped with the remaining curry leaves and olive oil.

TIP

If you like your egg yolks soft, add the four remaining unwhisked eggs halfway through the cooking time in step 4 instead of prior to frying in step 3.

Speedy white bean and pea pasta

FAST/GLUTEN-FREE/HIGH-FIBER | PREP + COOK TIME **20 MINUTES** | SERVES **4**

PER SERVING | Calories 556 | Carbohydrates 63g | Total sugars 7g | Fat 21g | Saturated fat 7g | Sodium 0.3g plus seasoning | Fiber 11g

Peas, beans, and legumes are good sources of fiber, protein, and carbohydrate, as well as
B vitamins and essential minerals such as iron, magnesium, and zinc. Regular intake may also
lower blood pressure and cholesterol levels, and even help with weight control. Who knew
that such a humble food group could have such a powerful effect on health?

1/2 lb (225g) gluten-free spaghetti

1/4 cup extra virgin olive oil, divided

1/2 cup finely chopped onion

2 garlic cloves, crushed

1 x 15 1/2 oz (400g) can cannellini beans, drained, rinsed

2 cups frozen peas

3/4 cup light sour cream

1 lemon

3/4 cup finely grated Parmesan cheese

1/4 cup finely chopped fresh dill, plus extra, for serving

salt and freshly ground black pepper

1 Cook the spaghetti in a large saucepan of boiling salted water for 8 minutes or until almost tender. Drain, reserving 3/4 cup of the cooking water.

2 Meanwhile, heat 2 tablespoons of the olive oil in a large nonstick skillet over medium heat. Cook the onion and garlic, covered, stirring occasionally, for 5 minutes until soft.

3 Add the white beans, peas, and sour cream; reduce the heat to low. Cook for 1 minute. Using a potato masher, crush the beans and peas over low heat until half of them are mashed; this will help to thicken the sauce. Cut the lemon in half. Juice one half; cut the remaining half into wedges. Add the Parmesan cheese, chopped dill, and 1 tablespoon of lemon juice to the bean mixture; season with salt and pepper to taste.

4 Add the hot pasta and reserved cooking water to the pan; cook, stirring, for 1 minute or until the pasta is coated in sauce. Drizzle with the remaining olive oil and sprinkle with the extra dill. Serve immediately with the lemon wedges for squeezing over.

Mushroom tofu burger in butternut "bun"

VEGETARIAN/HIGH-PROTEIN | PREP + COOK TIME **55 MINUTES + REFRIGERATION** | SERVES **4**
PER SERVING | Calories 783 | Carbohydrates 93g | Total sugars 38g | Fat 30g | Saturated fats 8g | Sodium 2g plus seasoning | Fiber 13g

Tofu is a great source of amino acids, iron, and calcium. It is super-versatile, too, making it a great meat substitute in these burgers; nutritionally empty white burger buns are replaced by butternut squash for a veggie-rich meal.

6 green onions, divided

12 oz (300g) extra-firm tofu, coarsely chopped

8 oz (200g) button mushrooms, coarsely chopped

2 garlic cloves, crushed

2 tbsp Dijon mustard

2 cups fresh whole-grain bread crumbs

1 egg

4¼ lb (2kg) butternut squash, unpeeled

¼ cup extra virgin olive oil

4 slices of Swiss cheese

1 head butter lettuce, leaves separated

1 large vine-ripened tomato, thinly sliced

¼ cup ketchup

1 tsp sesame seeds, toasted

salt and freshly ground black pepper

1   Finely chop three of the green onions. In the bowl of a food processor, add the green onions, tofu, mushrooms, garlic, mustard, bread crumbs, and egg. Pulse until the mixture comes together. Add salt and pepper to taste. Shape the mixture into four patties; cover and refrigerate for 20 minutes to firm.

2   Meanwhile, cut the unpeeled butternut squash in half widthwise; reserve the stem end for another use. Cut the remaining squash into eight ½ inch (1cm) rounds.

3   Heat 1 tablespoon of the olive oil in a large skillet over medium heat; cook half of the squash slices for 5 minutes on each side or until golden and cooked through. Drain on paper towels. Repeat with another 1 tablespoon of the olive oil and the remaining squash slices.

4   Cut the remaining green onions into 4¾ inch (12cm) lengths, then cut these lengths into thin shreds. Place in a bowl of iced water to curl. Set aside; drain before using.

5   Heat the remaining olive oil in the same frying pan over medium heat; cook the tofu patties for 2 minutes; turn over and cook for 1 minute. Top each patty with a slice of cheese, and cook for 1 minute longer or until golden and the cheese is starting to melt.

6   To assemble the burgers, place a squash round on each of four serving plates; top each one with lettuce, a tofu patty, tomato slices, ketchup, and some of the drained curled green onion tops. Sandwich each stack with one of the remaining squash slices; secure with short skewers. Sprinkle with the toasted sesame seeds.

TIP

Roast the leftover squash to use in salads or turn into butternut squash soup.

Sweet-potato-breaded sheet-pan fish

ONE-PAN | PREP + COOK TIME **35 MINUTES** | SERVES **4**
PER SERVING | Calories 640 | Carbohydrates 69g | Total sugars 23g | Fat 16g | Saturated fat 5g | Sodium 1g plus seasoning | Fiber 13g

White fish is an excellent source of iodine. A four-ounce (100g) portion, for example, provides you with more than a quarter of your daily requirements. Iodized salt (used to supplement dietary iodine) is not common in the UK and so iodine deficiency has re-emerged there. Iodine is essential for the production of thyroid hormones that control metabolism.

extra virgin olive oil cooking spray

2 lb (1kg) sweet potato, cut into ¾ in (2cm) pieces

¾ lb (400g) vine tomatoes

½ lb (250g) snow peas, trimmed

½ cup sliced almonds

¾ cup flat-leaf parsley leaves, divided, plus extra sprigs, to garnish (optional)

1 slice of stale whole-grain sourdough bread, well toasted, coarsely torn

4 x ½ lb (250g) skinless, firm white fish fillets

⅓ cup Greek yogurt

salt and freshly ground black pepper

1 lemon, cut into wedges, for serving

cocktail sauce

½ cup Greek yogurt

2 tbsp lemon juice

2 tsp creamy horseradish

extra virgin olive oil, to garnish (optional)

1 Preheat the oven to 425°F (220°C). Lightly oil a wire cooling rack with cooking spray, then place over a baking sheet. Line a second large baking sheet with parchment paper.

2 Reserve ¾ cup of the sweet potato for the breading; spread the remaining sweet potato over the parchment-paper-lined baking tray. Spray with the olive oil; season with salt and pepper to taste. Bake the sweet potato for 20 minutes or until golden. Reserve 2 tomatoes for the cocktail sauce; add the remaining tomatoes and snow peas to the tray. Spray with the olive oil; bake for 5 minutes longer.

3 Meanwhile, put the reserved sweet potato in a food processor with the almonds, ½ cup of the parsley leaves, and the toasted bread. Process to form coarse crumbs. Transfer to a medium bowl; season well with salt and a good grinding of pepper.

4 Place the fish on the prepared oiled rack. Using the back of a spoon, spread 1 tablespoon yogurt evenly over the top of each fish fillet. Press on the crumb mixture; spray with the olive oil. Bake for 12 minutes or until the crumb is golden and the fish is cooked through.

5 Meanwhile, to make the cocktail sauce, finely grate the reserved tomatoes from step 2; place in a bowl with the yogurt, lemon juice, and creamy horseradish. Mix well to combine; season with salt and pepper to taste. Drizzle with a little olive oil, if you like.

6 Toss the remaining parsley leaves into the roasted vegetables; top with the fish. Serve with the cocktail sauce, lemon wedges for squeezing over, and extra parsley sprigs, if you like.

Cauliflower and tofu curry

VEGETARIAN | PREP + COOK TIME **35 MINUTES** | SERVES **4**

PER SERVING | Calories 632 | Carbohydrates 29g | Total sugars 13g | Fat 42g | Saturated fat 21g | Sodium 0.3g plus seasoning | Fiber 12g

A plant-based curry is an easy way to increase your vegetable intake. Each of the vegetables here offers a unique array of nutrients. Garlic and shallots contain prebiotics called fructo-oligosaccharides, which, when included in our diet, promote the growth of healthy bacteria in the gut. This recipe does have a high amount of saturated fat, so make sure to reserve this dish for an otherwise lean day.

2 x 1½ in (4cm) pieces fresh ginger

¼ cup extra virgin olive oil, divided

8 shallots, halved

2 tbsp curry powder

1 tsp ground turmeric

1 x 13½ oz (400 ml) can light coconut cream

1 cup vegetable stock

½ large cauliflower, cut into large florets

1 lb (500g) firm tofu, cut into 1 in (2.5cm) pieces

1¼ cups frozen peas

⅓ cup curry leaves

2 garlic cloves, thinly sliced

salt and freshly ground black pepper

steamed brown rice, for serving

lime wedges, for serving

1 Peel the ginger; finely grate 1 piece of the ginger and thinly slice the remaining piece. Heat 1 tablespoon of the olive oil in a large, heavy-based saucepan over medium heat; cook the shallots, covered, for 2 minutes or until they start to soften and the edges turn golden.

2 Add the curry powder, turmeric, and grated ginger; cook, stirring, for 30 seconds until fragrant. Add the coconut cream and vegetable stock; cook, scraping the bottom of the pan with a wooden spoon, until well combined. Add the cauliflower and tofu; cook, covered, for 15 minutes or until the cauliflower is just tender, stirring halfway through the cooking time. Add the peas for the last 2 minutes of cooking time. Season with salt and pepper to taste.

3 Meanwhile, heat the remaining olive oil in a small, heavy-based saucepan over medium heat. Carefully add the sliced ginger, curry leaves, and garlic (the oil will splutter). Cook, stirring frequently, for 2 minutes or until the curry leaves are crisp. Stir half of the ginger mixture into the curry.

4 Top the curry with the remaining ginger mixture. Serve with steamed brown rice and lime wedges for squeezing over.

Vietnamese-style eggplant noodles

FAST | PREP + COOK TIME **30 MINUTES** | SERVES **4**

PER SERVING | Calories 365 | Carbohydrates 60g | Total sugars 17g | Fat 6g | Saturated fat 1g | Sodium 2.9g | Fiber 8g

To make this bold and vibrantly colored Vietnamese-inspired recipe vegetarian, swap the fish sauce with the same amount of dark soy sauce. Make sure you eat the noodles with a generous handful of herbs for the added freshness typical of Vietnamese cuisine.

1 lb (500g) globe eggplant, cut into ¾ in (2cm) pieces

½ lb (225g) fresh shiitake mushrooms, thinly sliced

2 shallots, thinly sliced, divided

1 tbsp fish sauce

1 tbsp honey

1 tbsp extra virgin olive oil

1½ tsp Chinese five-spice powder

½ lb (225g) dried brown rice vermicelli noodles

½ lb (250g) green beans, trimmed, halved lengthwise

extra virgin olive oil cooking spray

4 small rice paper rounds

2 tsp black sesame seeds

2 carrots, peeled, julienned

½ bunch of mint leaves, sprigs picked

nuoc cham

2 tbsp fish sauce

2½ tbsp white vinegar

1½ tbsp honey or coconut sugar

1 small red chile, finely chopped (optional)

1 Preheat the oven to 400°F (200°C). Line a baking sheet with parchment paper.

2 Put the eggplant, mushrooms, half of the sliced shallots, fish sauce, honey, olive oil, and Chinese five-spice in a large bowl; mix well to coat. Spread the vegetable mixture over the prepared tray; roast for 20 minutes, stirring halfway through the cooking time, or until the vegetables are golden brown.

3 Meanwhile, place the noodles and green beans in a large heat-safe bowl; cover with boiling water. Allow to stand for 5 minutes or until the noodles are soft. Drain and rinse under cold running water.

4 To make the nuoc cham, put the ingredients in a small saucepan; add ½ cup water. Stir over low heat until the honey dissolves and the mixture almost reaches a simmer. Set aside to keep warm.

5 Spray one rice paper round with olive oil cooking spray; sprinkle with ½ teaspoon of the sesame seeds. Microwave on high (100%) for 50 seconds or until puffed up and white. Repeat with the remaining rice papers and sesame seeds.

6 Divide the noodles, carrots, green beans, and eggplant mixture among four serving bowls; top with the mint sprigs and remaining shallots. Pour over the hot nuoc cham. Serve with the rice paper crackers.

Green curry steamed fish parcels

HIGH-PROTEIN/FAST | PREP + COOK TIME **30 MINUTES** | SERVES **4**
PER SERVING | Calories 408 | Carbohydrates 28g | Total sugars 9g | Fat 17g | Saturated fat 12g | Sodium 3.3g plus seasoning | Fiber 3g

Cooking fish in a paper parcel is a beautifully healthy way of preparing it. The aromatic cooking liquid flavors the fish while creating steam to cook it. This is a particularly good method for delicate white fish, which can fall apart with direct-heat cooking methods.

4 oz (100g) dried brown rice vermicelli noodles

¼ cup Thai green curry paste

1¼ cups coconut milk

2 tbsp fish sauce

1 tbsp light soft brown sugar

1 lb (500g) baby bok choy, cut into thirds

4 x 5 oz (150g) boneless firm white fish fillets, skin on

6 makrut lime leaves

½ cup Thai basil leaves, plus extra, for serving

1 long green chile, thinly sliced

lime wedges, for serving

1 Put the noodles in a heat-safe bowl; cover with boiling water. Let stand for 5 minutes until soft; drain well.

2 Mix together the curry paste, coconut milk, fish sauce, and brown sugar in a small bowl.

3 Place four 20 inch (51cm) lengths of aluminum foil on a work surface. Top each one with a sheet of parchment paper half the size, placed at one end of the foil.

4 Divide the bok choy, fish, and four of the makrut lime leaves equally among each piece of parchment paper, positioning in the center. Slowly pour one-quarter of the green curry mixture over each piece of fish and top with the basil leaves. Bring the foil up and over the filling, and fold the edges to seal and form a half-moon shape.

5 Place the parcels in a large bamboo steamer over a wok of simmering water; cover with a lid. Steam the parcels for 15 minutes or until the fish is cooked through.

6 Shred the remaining lime leaves. Carefully open the parcels; add the drained noodles. Serve immediately, sprinkled with chile, extra Thai basil leaves, shredded lime leaves, and lime wedges for squeezing over.

TIP

If you don't have a large bamboo steamer, preheat the oven to 350°F (180°C). Place the parcels on a large baking sheet; bake for 20 minutes.

Oven-baked gluten-free breaded chicken with pea purée

GLUTEN-FREE/HIGH-FIBER | PREP **35 MINUTES** | SERVES **4**

PER SERVING | Calories 518 | Carbohydrates 24g | Total sugars 7g | Fat 21g | Saturated fat 4g | Sodium 0.4g plus seasoning | Fiber 8g

Quinoa and almonds are both used to make the nutritious coating for the chicken.
Quinoa is rich in several B group vitamins required to turn the food you eat into energy
to fuel your body, while almonds are head and shoulders above other nuts for vitamin E.

extra virgin olive oil cooking spray

$^2/_3$ cup quinoa flakes

$^1/_3$ cup natural almonds, finely chopped

$^1/_3$ cup finely grated Parmesan cheese

1 egg, lightly beaten

2 x $^1/_2$lb (300g) boneless, skinless chicken breasts, halved lengthwise

10 oz (300g) cherry tomatoes

4 cups frozen peas, thawed

2 cups basil leaves, divided

2 tbsp extra virgin olive oil

salt and freshly ground black pepper

1 small lemon, cut into wedges, for serving

1   Preheat the oven to 425°F (220°C). Line a baking sheet with parchment paper. Top with a wire cooling rack. Spray the cooking rack with cooking spray.

2   Put the quinoa flakes, almonds, and Parmesan cheese on a large plate; stir to mix evenly. Season well with salt and a good grinding of pepper. Put the beaten egg in a separate shallow bowl. Dip the chicken into the egg, then press it into the quinoa mixture to coat.

3   Place the chicken on the prepared rack over the baking sheet; spray with the cooking spray. Bake for 20 minutes, turning halfway through the cooking time. Add the tomatoes to the baking sheet; bake for 5 minutes longer or until the tomatoes blister and the chicken is golden brown.

4   Meanwhile, make the pea puree. In the bowl of a food processor, add the peas, 1$^1/_2$ cups of the basil, and the olive oil; process, stopping to scrape down the sides, for 2 minutes or until smooth. Season with salt and pepper to taste.

5   Serve the chicken with the pea purée, blistered tomatoes, and lemon wedges for squeezing over; top with the remaining basil leaves.

CROWD-PLEASING

Looking for inspiration for a celebration feast or leisurely lunch? Wondering how to feed any unexpected extras at the dinner table? These recipes have you covered.

Smoky red lentil meatless loaf

VEGETARIAN | PREP + COOK TIME **1 HOUR 20 MINUTES + OVERNIGHT STANDING** | SERVES **4**
PER SERVING | Calories 734 | Carbohydrates 72g | Total sugars 29g | Fat 31g | Saturated fat 13g | Sodium 1.9g plus seasoning | Fiber 13g

This plant-based loaf has the heartiness of meatloaf without the meat, so it's a filling meal
for those days when you need comfort food. Leftovers can be toasted in a sandwich press and
served piled onto whole-grain bread, with lettuce leaves and a little tomato chutney.

You will need to soak the lentils 8 hours ahead

1¼ cups dried red lentils

2 tbsp extra virgin olive oil, plus extra for greasing

½ cup finely chopped onion

2 garlic cloves, finely chopped

¼ cup oregano leaves, finely chopped

1 tsp smoked paprika

1 carrot

1 lb (500g) parsnips

3 eggs, lightly beaten

½ cup vegetable stock

1½ cups grated Cheddar cheese, divided

salt and freshly ground black pepper

6 cups mixed salad leaves, for serving

1 cup chipotle ketchup or tomato chutney, for serving

1 Put the lentils in a large bowl; cover with cold water. Let stand for 8 hours or overnight. Drain; rinse under cold water, then drain well.

2 Preheat the oven to 400°F (200°C). Line the bottom and sides of a 9 inch (23cm) loaf pan with parchment paper.

3 Heat the olive oil in a medium frying pan over medium heat. Cook the onion, garlic, and oregano, stirring occasionally, for 5 minutes or until softened. Stir in the paprika. Set aside to cool.

4 Meanwhile, scrub the carrot and parsnips; leave unpeeled. Thinly slice half of one parsnip lengthwise. Coarsely grate the remaining parsnip and the carrot. Combine the grated vegetables, beaten eggs, vegetable stock, 1¼ cups of the Cheddar cheese, lentils, and onion mixture in a large bowl; season with salt and pepper to taste. Spoon the mixture into the prepared pan; spread and level the mixture using the back of a spoon. Top with the sliced parsnip; sprinkle with the remaining Cheddar cheese. Cover with aluminum foil greased with a little olive oil. Scrunch the foil around the sides of the pan to secure it.

5 Bake the loaf for 30 minutes. Remove the foil; bake 30 minutes longer or until golden.

6 Let the loaf stand in the pan for 5 minutes before turning it out, top side up, onto a board. Cool for 15 minutes before slicing. Serve with the salad leaves and the chipotle ketchup or chutney.

TIP

You can pan-fry slices of the lentil loaf to serve in a burger bun, for a vegetarian burger patty.

Black barley pilaf and roasted sweet potato

VEGETARIAN | PREP + COOK TIME **1 HOUR 30 MINUTES** | SERVES **6**

PER SERVING | Calories 663 | Carbohydrates 95g | Total sugars 22g | Fat 23g | Saturated fat 6g | Sodium 0.9g plus seasoning | Fiber 11g

Black barley has the bran layer intact, and is super nutritious with a pleasant, chewy texture and a nutty taste. The dark pigment in it—anthocyanin—is also found in blueberries and other dark purple or black foods. It has anti-inflammatory properties.

6 sweet potatoes

1/3 cup extra virgin olive oil, divided

1/2 cup finely chopped onion

1 tbsp ground cumin

1 cup black barley (see tip)

2 cups vegetable stock

1/4 cup dried cranberries, chopped

1/2 cup coarsely chopped flat-leaf parsley, plus extra 1/3 cup firmly packed flat-leaf parsley leaves, for serving

1/2 cup pistachios, chopped

4 oz (125g) soft feta cheese, crumbled

salt and freshly ground black pepper to taste

1 Preheat the oven to 350°F (180°C). Line a baking sheet with parchment paper.

2 Scrub the sweet potatoes; leave unpeeled, but cut in half lengthwise. Arrange the sweet potatoes, cut-side up, on the prepared tray; drizzle with 2 tablespoons of the olive oil; season with salt and pepper to taste. Bake for 1 hour or until tender.

3 Meanwhile, heat 1 tablespoon of the olive oil in a large saucepan over medium heat. Add the onion; cook, stirring occasionally, for 5 minutes or until the onion softens. Add the cumin; stir for 30 seconds until fragrant. Add the barley; stir to mix through evenly. Add the stock; bring to a boil. Reduce the heat to low; cook, covered, for 40 minutes or until almost all the liquid has been absorbed and the barley is tender. Remove from the heat; stir in the cranberries and chopped parsley.

4 Remove the flesh in the center of the sweet potatoes with a spoon, leaving a 1/2 inch (1cm) shell. Cut the scooped flesh into pieces.

5 Spoon the pilaf mixture into the sweet potato shells, mounding it slightly. Top with the sweet potato pieces, pistachios, and crumbled feta cheese. Bake for 10 minutes or until the filling is heated through and the feta cheese is a light golden color.

6 Serve the sweet potatoes drizzled with the remaining olive oil and topped with the extra parsley leaves.

TIP

If black barley is unavailable, substitute regular barley or farro.

Mushroom and sweet corn soft tacos

HEALTHY FATS | PREP + COOK TIME **40 MINUTES** | SERVES **4**

PER SERVING | Calories 633 | Carbohydrates 41g | Total sugars 11g | Fat 38g | Saturated fat 9g | Sodium 2.2g plus seasoning | Fiber 11g

Mushrooms are rich in B vitamins and fiber, while the cottage cheese and black bean salsa contribute protein. Avocados are a surprisingly good source of vitamin C. This makes them a great addition to a vegetarian meal, as they will help you to absorb more plant iron.

10 oz (300g) firm tofu, drained

3 large portobello mushroom caps, chopped

8 oz (225g) white button mushrooms, cleaned, halved

8 oz (225g) mixed wild mushrooms including oyster, chanterelle, and shiitake, cleaned and chopped

1¼ cups black bean and chipotle salsa (see tips)

½ bunch of cilantro

2 tbsp extra virgin olive oil, divided, plus extra for drizzling (optional)

1 cup fresh or frozen corn

8 x 6 in (15cm) white corn or flour tortillas

1 cup cottage cheese

2 avocados

4 oz (120g) cherry tomatoes, quartered

salt and freshly ground black pepper

1 Crumble the tofu into a large bowl, forming a mixture of large and small chunks. Add the mushrooms, salsa, and 2 tablespoons of the cilantro; stir well to mix evenly.

2 Heat 1 tablespoon of the olive oil in a large, heavy nonstick skillet over high heat. Add half of the mushroom mixture; cook, stirring occasionally, for 8 minutes or until the mushrooms are browned and tender. Transfer to a bowl. Repeat with the remaining olive oil and the mushroom mixture. Add all of the mushrooms to the skillet and add the corn. Stir to heat. Season with salt and pepper to taste. Remove the pan from the heat; cover to keep warm.

3 Meanwhile, preheat a ridged cast-iron grill pan over medium heat. Cook the tortillas, one at a time, for 30 seconds on each side or until grill marks appear. Transfer to a plate; keep warm.

4 Slice each avocado in half and remove the pit. Scoop the flesh into the bowl of a food processor. Add the cottage cheese and process until smooth. Season with salt and pepper to taste.

5 Stir ½ cup of cilantro into the mushroom mixture; divide evenly among the tortillas. Top with the tomatoes and remaining cilantro. Serve the tacos with the avocado-cottage cheese, drizzled with extra olive oil, if you like.

TIPS

- If you like things spicy, add a pinch of dried chili flakes or sliced fresh chile to the mushrooms.
- If you can't find black bean and chipotle salsa, make your own by mixing a smoky chipotle salsa with some drained black beans.

Oven-baked veggie sesame tempura with soba noodles

VEGETARIAN | PREP + COOK TIME **25 MINUTES** | SERVES **4**

PER SERVING | Calories 652 | Carbohydrates 93g | Total sugars 14g | Fat 19g | Saturated fat 3g | Sodium 3.6g plus seasoning | Fiber 9g

Soba noodles are a low-GI Japanese noodle made from a mixture of buckwheat and wheat, making them both high in dietary fiber and a complete protein. The sodium content is high; however, it reduces significantly after cooking.

8 oz (225g) buckwheat soba noodles

1 tbsp sesame oil

1/2 cup toasted sesame seeds, crushed, plus extra 1 tbsp

2/3 cup rice flour

2 tsp sea salt flakes

5 egg whites, lightly whisked until frothy

6 oz (170g) broccolini, trimmed, blanched (see tip)

5 oz (150g) oyster mushrooms

10 oz (300g) butternut squash, seeds and strings scooped out, thinly sliced, skin on

ginger dressing

1 1/2 tbsp tamari

1/3 cup mirin rice cooking wine

1/4 cup pink pickled ginger, plus 2 tbsp of the pickling liquid

1 tsp sesame oil

3 tbsp thinly sliced cucumber

1 green onion, thinly sliced

salt and freshly ground black pepper to taste

TIP

To blanch the broccolini, place in a heat-safe bowl; pour boiling water over it. Let stand until bright green. Drain; then refresh under cold running water. Pat dry with paper towels.

1 Cook the noodles in a large saucepan of boiling water for 3 minutes or until just tender. Drain and refresh under cold running water until cool; toss with the sesame oil. Set aside.

2 Preheat the oven to 425°F (220°C). Line 2 large baking sheets with parchment paper.

3 Put the sesame seeds, rice flour, and sea salt flakes in a shallow bowl; stir to combine. Put the whisked egg whites in a second shallow bowl.

4 Working in batches, dip the broccolini, mushrooms, and butternut squash slices into the egg white, then into the flour mixture, shaking to remove any excess. Place on the prepared pans. Bake for 10 minutes, flipping the vegetables over halfway through cooking. Bake until crisp and golden.

5 Meanwhile, to make the ginger dressing, put the tamari, mirin, pickling liquid, and sesame oil in a screw-top jar with a tight-fitting lid; shake well. Season with salt and pepper to taste. Transfer to a small bowl; stir in the cucumber, green onion, and pickled ginger.

6 Arrange the noodles evenly divided over 4 serving plates. Drizzle half of the dressing over the noodles. Top with the tempura vegetables. Serve with the remaining dressing, sprinkled with the extra 1 tablespoon sesame seeds.

Chicken, broccoli pesto, and chickpea pasta

HIGH-PROTEIN | PREP + COOK TIME **30 MINUTES** | SERVES **4**

PER SERVING | Calories 722 | Carbohydrates 66g | Total sugars 4g | Fat 28g | Saturated fat 6g | Sodium 0.4g plus seasoning | Fiber 9g

Pastas made with wheat alternatives are a terrific way to boost your intake of plant-based food. You'll find them made of chickpeas, lentils, legumes, or a combination of lentils and quinoa. The benefit is a more filling and nutritious pasta.

³/₄ lb (400g) skinless, boneless chicken breasts

12 oz (340g) dried chickpea pasta

10 oz (300g) broccoli, coarsely chopped

1 cup firmly packed basil leaves, plus extra to garnish

¹/₂ cup pistachios, roasted

1 garlic clove, crushed

¹/₂ cup finely grated Parmesan cheese

¹/₃ cup extra virgin olive oil

¹/₃ cup lemon juice

1 tsp finely grated lemon zest

2 cups shredded curly kale

salt and freshly ground black pepper

1 lemon, cut into wedges, for serving

1 In a medium pot, add the chicken and enough cold water to cover. Bring to a boil, then reduce the heat to a gentle simmer; poach for 10 minutes or until thoroughly cooked. Allow to cool; coarsely shred.

2 Meanwhile, cook the pasta in a large pot of salted boiling water for 6 minutes or until almost tender; drain. Return the pasta to the pot.

3 At the same time, in a food processor, add the broccoli, basil, pistachios, garlic, Parmesan cheese, olive oil, lemon juice, and lemon zest until smooth. Season with salt and pepper to taste.

4 Combine the chicken, kale, and pesto with the pasta in the pan. Season with salt and pepper to taste; toss well. Sprinkle the pasta with the extra basil leaves; serve with the lemon wedges for squeezing over.

Spicy fish skewers with broccoli rice

HIGH-PROTEIN | PREP + COOK TIME **35 MINUTES + REFRIGERATION** | SERVES **4**

PER SERVING | Calories 478 | Carbohydrates 10g | Total sugars 5g | Fat 23g | Saturated fat 4g | Sodium 1.2g plus seasoning | Fiber 7g

Oily fish such as sardines, salmon, and mackerel often get all the kudos, but white fish do provide a wealth of other nutrients even if they don't contain omega-3 fats. They are protein-rich, with a 3½-ounce (100g) fillet providing you with 20g of high-quality protein.

1½ cups chopped cilantro, plus extra leaves for serving

1 cup chopped roasted red peppers

2 tbsp chipotle in adobo sauce

2 garlic cloves, crushed

¼ cup pine nuts, toasted

2 tbsp sunflower seeds

1 tbsp flax seeds

1 tbsp sesame seeds

1 tsp ground cumin

2 tbsp extra virgin olive oil

2 lbs (1 kg) skinless firm white fish fillets, cut into 1¼ in (3cm) pieces

1½ tbsp lemon juice

2 large zucchini, thinly sliced lengthwise

salt and freshly ground black pepper

broccoli rice

¾ lb (400g) head of broccoli, trimmed and cut into florets

2 tbsp extra virgin olive oil

1 In the bowl of a food processor, combine ⅓ cup of the cilantro, the roasted red peppers, chipotle in adobo, garlic, pine nuts, sunflower seeds, flax seeds, and sesame seeds. Pulse until they form a paste. Season with salt and pepper to taste.

2 Put the fish pieces in a large bowl, and add half of the pepper paste; toss to coat. Cover and refrigerate for 10 minutes. Stir the lemon juice into the remaining pepper paste to make the dressing; set aside.

3 Meanwhile, to make the broccoli rice, place the broccoli in the bowl of a food processor and pulse until it resembles grains of rice. Heat the olive oil in a large skillet over medium heat; cook the broccoli for 2 minutes or until bright green and softened slightly. Stir in ¾ cup of the reserved cilantro leaves. Season with salt and pepper to taste.

4 Thread the fish onto 8 metal or soaked bamboo skewers, alternating it with the zucchini ribbons. Preheat an oiled ridged cast-iron grill pan over high heat; cook the skewers, turning, for 8 minutes or until just cooked through and grill marks appear.

5 Serve the skewers with the broccoli rice, topped with the roasted red pepper seed dressing and the remaining reserved cilantro and reserved leaves.

TIPS

• Slice the zucchini into ribbons with a vegetable peeler, mandoline, or V-slicer.

• If using bamboo skewers, before use soak them in boiling water for 10 minutes.

Shrimp and sweet potato panang curry

HIGH-PROTEIN | PREP + COOK TIME **30 MINUTES** | SERVES **4**

PER SERVING | Calories 539 | Carbohydrates 55g | Total sugars 18g | Fat 21g | Saturated fat 8g | Sodium 2.6g | Fiber 10g

For years people worried about the cholesterol found in shrimp. Today, we understand much more about what dietary factors affect our blood cholesterol profile. Dietary cholesterol is a minor factor. If you have high cholesterol, concentrate on changing the types of fat in your diet rather than worrying about cholesterol in food.

1/4 cup Thai red curry paste

1/2 cup thinly sliced red onion

3 in (8cm) piece of fresh ginger, grated

2 sweet potatoes, cut into 1/4 inch thick rounds

1/4 cup smooth peanut butter

1 x 13 1/2 oz (400ml) can light coconut milk

2 cups vegetable stock

3/4 lb (400g) medium raw shrimp, peeled, tails on

3/4 lb (350g) snow peas, cut into thirds

1 tbsp fish sauce

1 tbsp lime juice

1 tbsp pure maple syrup

1/2 cup firmly packed cilantro leaves, divided

2 green onions, shredded

1 Put the curry paste, onion, and ginger in a large, heavy saucepan over low heat. Cook, covered, stirring occasionally, for 10 minutes or until the onion is softened.

2 Increase the heat to medium; stir in the sweet potato, peanut butter, coconut milk, and vegetable stock until combined. Bring to a simmer; cook, covered, for 15 minutes or until a sharp knife can be inserted into the sweet potato without resistance.

3 Add the shrimp and snow peas to the curry; cook, uncovered, for 3 minutes longer or until the shrimp are just cooked through. Stir in the fish sauce, lime juice, maple syrup, and 1/4 cup of the cilantro.

4 Serve the curry evenly divided among 4 serving bowls, topped with the shredded green onions and the remaining cilantro leaves.

TIP

Serve with steamed brown and wild rice and coarsely chopped salted roasted peanuts.

Quick inside-out roast chicken

HIGH-PROTEIN | PREP + COOK TIME **1 HOUR 5 MINUTES** | SERVES **4**

PER SERVING | Calories 690 | Carbohydrates 41g | Total sugars 15g | Fat 25g | Saturated fat 5g | Sodium 2.1g plus seasoning | Fiber 11g

One of the challenges of cooking a whole chicken is that the breast and leg meat require different cooking times. Add in a stuffing and you further increase the chances of dry breast meat. Roasting the stuffing outside of the chicken solves the problem.

1 whole roasting chicken (about 4 lb [1.8kg])

½ cup firmly packed sage leaves

¼ cup extra virgin olive oil, divided, plus 1 tsp extra

2 carrots, trimmed

1 large onion

1 cup rolled (old-fashioned) oats

3 slices whole-grain bread

¼ cup golden raisins

1 tsp sea salt flakes

1 large lemon, halved

¾ lb (400g) green beans, trimmed

1 tsp finely grated lemon zest

salt and freshly ground black pepper

1 Preheat the oven to 400°F (200°C).

2 Place the chicken, breast-side down, on a cutting board. Using a pair of kitchen scissors, cut along both sides of the backbone, then remove it; reserve the backbone. Press down lightly on the chicken legs to open the chicken out flat. Using a large, sharp knife, cut down through the breastbone and skin to halve the chicken.

3 Place the chicken backbone in the center of the roasting pan; place the chicken, skin-side up, on top of the backbone. Rub with 1 tablespoon of the olive oil; season with salt and pepper to taste. Sprinkle with half of the sage leaves.

4 In a food processor, combine the carrots, onion, oats, bread, golden raisins, sea salt flakes, and the remaining sage and olive oil; process until finely chopped and the mixture holds together when pressed. Divide the stuffing evenly into 8 large balls; arrange the stuffing and the lemon halves around the chicken in the roasting pan.

5 Bake the chicken and stuffing for 50 minutes or until the chicken is golden and cooked through. Let the chicken rest, loosely covered in aluminum foil, for 10 minutes.

6 Meanwhile, put the green beans on a parchment-paper-lined baking sheet; toss with the extra 1 teaspoon oil. Season with salt and pepper to taste. Cook on the top rack of the oven for 10 minutes.

7 Serve the chicken with the stuffing, green beans, and lemon halves, sprinkled with the lemon zest.

TIP

If you like, line a 9in x 13in (24cm x 32cm) roasting pan with a large piece of parchment paper before adding the chicken. This makes for easier cleanup once the cooking is done.

Roast veggies

Roasting brings out the natural sweetness in vegetables—particularly root vegetables—heightening their flavor and transforming them into irresistible bundles of yumminess for your taste buds. And all the while you still gain the benefits of their nutrients and fiber.

Parsnip and apple

PREP + COOK TIME **40 MINUTES** | SERVES **4**

Preheat the oven to 400°F (200°C). Scrub and trim 2 lb (1kg) parsnips and core 2 Red Delicious or Gala apples. Cut the parsnips lengthwise into wedges. Cut the apples into wedges and remove the cores. Line a baking sheet with parchment paper. Arrange the parsnips and apples on the tray. Drizzle with 2 tablespoons each of honey and extra virgin olive oil, then add 6 small sprigs of rosemary. Season with salt and freshly ground black pepper to taste; toss to coat. Roast for 30 minutes or until the parsnips and apples are tender and browned. Add 2 slices of torn prosciutto; roast for 5 minutes longer or until crisp.

Squash and chickpeas

PREP + COOK TIME **45 MINUTES** | SERVES **4**

Preheat the oven to 425°F (220°C). Cut 2 lb (1kg) kabocha squash, leaving the skin on, lengthwise into wedges. Cut 2 red onions into wedges. Drain a 15 oz (425g) can of chickpeas; rinse. Place the squash, onion, chickpeas, and 10 torn thyme sprigs on a baking sheet lined with parchment paper. Drizzle with 1/4 cup extra virgin olive oil. Season with salt and freshly ground black pepper to taste; toss to coat. Roast for 40 minutes or until the squash is tender and browned. Serve tossed with arugula, if you like.

Beet and almond crumble

PREP + COOK TIME **1 HOUR** | SERVES **4**

Preheat the oven to 425°F (220°C). Trim the tops from 2 lb (1kg) red baby beets and 1 lb (500g) yellow baby beets; wash. Peel the red beets; cut in half. Keep the yellow ones whole and unpeeled. Place the red and golden beets on separate sheets of aluminum foil on a baking sheet. Add a bay leaf to each packet; drizzle each packet with 1 tablespoon olive oil. Cover each packet with another piece of foil to make parcels; seal. Roast the red beets for 40 minutes and the yellow beets for 30 minutes or until tender. Carefully peel the yellow beets; halve if large. In a food processor, combine 1/2 cup roasted natural almonds and 1/4 cup flat-leaf parsley until chopped. Sprinkle the roasted beet with the almond crumble.

Heirloom carrots

PREP + COOK TIME **40 MINUTES** | SERVES **6**

Preheat the oven to 400°F (200°C). Scrub 2 lb (1kg) each of orange, white, and purple heirloom carrots. Trim the stalks to 3/4 in (2cm) long, reserving the carrot tops. Pick 1 cup small, tender leaves from the reserved carrot tops; wash. Discard the remaining tops. In a food processor, combine the carrot top leaves with 1/2 cup extra virgin olive oil, 1/4 cup red wine vinegar, 1 tablespoon honey, and 2 teaspoons cumin seeds; process until finely chopped. Season with salt and freshly ground black pepper to taste. Drizzle half of the dressing over the carrots; roast for 30 minutes or until tender. Serve topped with the remaining dressing.

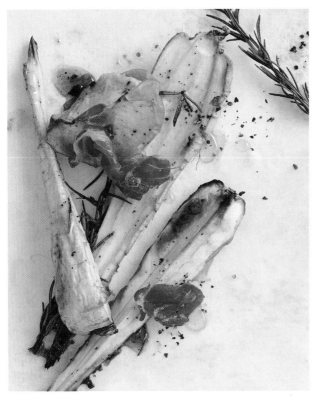

Cauliflower and chicken yogurt tandoori rice

GLUTEN-FREE | PREP + COOK TIME **40 MINUTES** | SERVES **4**

PER SERVING | Calories 854 | Carbohydrates 60g | Total sugars 15g | Fat 42g | Saturated fat 10g | Sodium 1.9g plus seasoning | Fiber 11g

It is easy to single out individual ingredients for their attributes, but to capture maximum nutrients it is important to eat from a wide array of food groups. Increasingly, evidence shows that it may be good for gut health, too.

1 cauliflower

1¼ lb (600g) chicken tenderloins

4 oz (125g) tandoori paste

1 cup Greek yogurt, divided

¼ cup extra virgin olive oil, divided

4 green onions, cut into 1¼ in (3cm) lengths

1 cup red quinoa

8¾ oz (250g) cooked brown rice

2½ cups vegetable stock

¼ cup unsalted cashews

1 cucumber, thinly sliced into rounds

1 cup cilantro leaves

salt and freshly ground black pepper to taste

1   Preheat the oven to 425°F (220°C). In a small bowl, combine the tandoori paste and ½ cup of the yogurt.

2   Cut the cauliflower into quarters, keeping the pale green leaves attached. Trim off a little of the central core, but not too much because you want to keep the florets attached; discard the core. Put the cauliflower quarters and chicken in a large bowl. Add the tandoori paste mixture; mix well until evenly coated.

3   Heat 2 tablespoons of the olive oil in a deep 12 in (30cm) Dutch oven or roasting pan over medium heat. Add the green onions and quinoa; cook, stirring, for 2 minutes or until the quinoa starts to crackle.

4   Add the rice and vegetable stock; lightly season with salt and pepper. Arrange the chicken, then the cauliflower, over the quinoa mixture, ensuring the cauliflower florets are on top and facing upward.

5   Transfer the rice mixture to the oven; bake uncovered for 20 minutes. Reduce the oven temperature to 400°F (200°C). Sprinkle with the cashews; bake 10 minutes longer or until the cauliflower tops are golden and the stock has been absorbed.

6   Top with the sliced cucumber, cilantro leaves, and remaining olive oil. Serve with the remaining yogurt.

TIP

To make the recipe vegetarian, replace the chicken with the same weight of firm tofu.

Turkish oven-roasted beans

VEGETARIAN/HIGH-FIBER | PREP + COOK TIME **50 MINUTES** | SERVES **4**

PER SERVING | Calories 816 | Carbohydrates 96g | Total sugars 16g | Fat 24g | Saturated fat 11g | Sodium 3.7g plus seasoning | Fiber 24g

Pomegranate molasses adds a sweet–sour flavor to this recipe. Also known as pomegranate syrup, its roots lie in Persian cuisine. If you don't have pomegranate molasses, replace it with 2 teaspoons of balsamic vinegar combined with 2 teaspoons of pure maple syrup.

1 large fennel bulb

2 tbsp extra virgin olive oil, divided

1 tsp ground allspice

2 tsp cumin seeds, divided

1 x 14¹/₂ oz (411g) can crushed tomatoes

2 x 15 oz (425g) cans butter beans, drained, rinsed

2 tbsp pomegranate molasses

8 oz (225g) haloumi cheese, sliced

¹/₄ cup firmly packed flat-leaf parsley leaves

salt and freshly ground black pepper

4 whole-grain pita bread pockets, halved, toasted, for serving

1 Preheat the oven to 425°F (220°C). Cut the fennel bulb into ½ inch (1cm) wedges; slice the green stalks into ¾ inch (2cm) slices.

2 Spread the fennel wedges and chopped stalks in a single layer on the bottom of a large roasting pan. Drizzle with 1 tablespoon of the olive oil. Sprinkle with the allspice and 1 teaspoon of the cumin seeds. Season with salt and pepper to taste.

3 Roast the fennel mixture for 15 minutes or until the edges start to brown.

4 Stir in the tomatoes, lima beans, and pomegranate molasses. Place the haloumi cheese over the top. Drizzle with the remaining olive oil; sprinkle with the remaining cumin seeds. Roast for 25 minutes or until the haloumi cheese is golden brown.

5 Sprinkle with the parsley leaves, and serve with the toasted pita bread.

One-pan vegetable, olive, and herb filo pie

VEGETARIAN/ONE-PAN | PREP + COOK TIME **45 MINUTES** | SERVES **4**
PER SERVING | Energy kcals 634 | Carbohydrate 52g of which sugar 7g | Fat 36g of which saturates 9g | Salt 3.8g plus seasoning | Fibre 6g

Swiss chard is high in non-haem iron, which is important in a vegetarian diet. Iron from plant
sources is not absorbed as well as haem iron from meat. Including vitamin C either in the dish
(we used tomatoes in this recipe) or with the meal as a whole can aid absorption.

¼ cup (60ml) extra virgin olive oil

350g chestnut mushrooms, halved

2 tbsp lemon thyme leaves, finely chopped,
plus extra 8 sprigs

4 garlic cloves, crushed

1 cup (180g) pitted Sicilian green olives

400g can diced tomatoes

500g Swiss chard, trimmed, coarsely chopped

⅓ cup (50g) pine nuts, toasted

150g haloumi, coarsely grated

6 sheets of filo pastry (thawed if frozen)

¼ cup (50g) couscous

salt and freshly ground black pepper

1 Preheat the oven to 220°C (200°C fan/425°F/Gas 7).

2 Heat 2 teaspoons of the olive oil in a 22cm (base measurement) deep ovenproof frying pan over a high heat. Cook the mushrooms, chopped lemon thyme, and garlic, stirring occasionally, for 5 minutes or until the mushrooms are golden. Season with salt and pepper to taste.

3 Coarsely chop three-quarters of the olives; leave the rest whole.

4 Add the tomatoes and chopped olives to pan with the mushrooms; cook for 5 minutes or until thickened. Add the Swiss chard; cook, stirring, for 1 minute or until wilted. Transfer to a large bowl; season with salt and pepper to taste. Set aside to cool. Wipe the pan clean and reserve. Finely chop ¼ cup of the pine nuts; combine with the haloumi in a small bowl.

5 Lightly brush the reserved pan with some of the remaining olive oil. Unwrap the filo and cover any sheets you aren't using immediately with baking parchment, then a damp tea towel. Lightly brush 1 sheet of filo with olive oil, and sprinkle with 2 tablespoons of the haloumi mixture. Top with a second sheet of filo. Repeat with the olive oil, haloumi mixture, and filo to create a stack of 3 sheets. Place in the frying pan, with the edges of the filo overhanging. Repeat with the remaining filo, olive oil, and haloumi mixture to create a second stack; place crossways in the frying pan. Sprinkle over the remaining haloumi mixture and the uncooked couscous.

6 Squeeze any excess liquid from the mushroom mixture. Spoon the cooled mushroom mixture into the pan. Fold over the filo to cover most of the pie, leaving a 6cm uncovered round in the centre for steam to escape. Brush the pastry top with the remaining oil. Set the pan on an oven tray.

7 Bake the pie for 18 minutes; top with the extra thyme sprigs and bake for a further 2 minutes or until golden. Serve topped with the remaining olives and pine nuts.

Broccoli and paneer saag curry

VEGETARIAN | PREP + COOK TIME **40 MINUTES** | SERVES **4**

PER SERVING | Calories 567 | Carbohydrates 21g | Total sugars 14g | Fat 32g | Saturated fat 17g | Sodium 0.4g | Fiber 13g

Paneer is a fresh cheese popular in Indian cooking and sold ready to eat in small pieces. It is rich in protein, with $3\frac{1}{2}$ ounces (100g) of paneer providing on average 18.3g of protein. If you are dairy-intolerant, substitute the same weight of firm tofu for the paneer.

2 tbsp extra virgin olive oil, divided

$^3/_4$ lb (400g) paneer, cut into $^3/_4$ in (2cm) pieces

$1^3/_4$ lb (800g) broccoli, cut into florets, divided

$^1/_2$ cup finely chopped onion

1 large bunch of cilantro, divided, with extra leaves reserved, to garnish

2 tbsp grated fresh ginger

2 tsp garam masala

1 x $14^1/_2$ oz (411g) can diced tomatoes

$2^1/_2$ cups vegetable stock

1 bunch of spinach, washed, leaves picked

10 oz (300g) sugar snap peas

2 tbsp lemon juice

1   Heat 1 tablespoon of the olive oil in a large, deep skillet over high heat. Cook the paneer, turning, for 3 minutes or until golden on all sides. Transfer to a large bowl. Cook 1 lb (500g) of the broccoli for 3 minutes or until browned; add to the bowl with the paneer.

2   Reduce the heat to medium. Heat the remaining olive oil in the same pan; cook the onion, $^1/_2$ cup of the cilantro, ginger, and garam masala for 5 minutes or until softened. Add the tomatoes and vegetable stock; bring to a boil. Cook for 8 minutes or until the stock has reduced slightly.

3   In the bowl of a food processor, pulse the remaining broccoli, remaining cilantro, and spinach leaves until finely chopped. Stir into the curry.

4   Return the paneer and cooked broccoli to the pan, along with the snow peas; cook for 3 minutes or until warmed through. Stir in the lemon juice.

5   Serve the curry topped with the reserved cilantro leaves.

TIP

Serve the curry with crisp whole-wheat flatbreads or brown rice, if you like.

Roasted mussels, tomatoes, and lima beans

HIGH-PROTEIN | PREP + COOK TIME **40 MINUTES** | SERVES **4**

PER SERVING | Calories 454 | Carbohydrates 48g | Total sugars 10g | Fat 9g | Saturated fat 1.5g | Sodium 2.7g plus seasoning | Fiber 6g

A dozen mussels provide all the iron and vitamin B12 you need for the day, a third of your zinc, more than a third of your magnesium, and a tenth of your vitamin A—and all for very few calories and pretty much no saturated fat. Most of those calories come from protein, so opting for mussels can help to curb your appetite.

1 x 28 oz (793 g) can crushed tomatoes

$^1/_3$ cup capers, drained

5 garlic cloves, thinly sliced, divided

1 tsp smoked paprika

$2^1/_2$ cups coarsely torn sourdough bread

$^1/_2$ tsp dried chili flakes

$^1/_4$ cup finely chopped flat-leaf parsley, plus extra sprigs, to garnish

1 tbsp extra virgin olive oil

3 lb (1.3kg) pot-ready mussels

1 x 15$^1/_2$ oz (439g) can lima beans, drained, rinsed

$2^1/_2$ cups firmly packed baby spinach leaves

salt and freshly ground black pepper

1 Preheat the oven to 425°F (220°C). Put the tomatoes, capers, 4 of the garlic cloves, and paprika in a large, deep-sided, heavy roasting pan. Cover with aluminum foil; cook for 20 minutes.

2 Meanwhile, put the torn bread, chili, parsley, and remaining garlic clove on a baking sheet; drizzle with the oil. Season with salt and pepper to taste; toss well to combine. Set aside.

3 Discard any mussels with broken shells and remove any beards.

4 Remove the foil from the roasting pan. Add the mussels and lima beans; stir to combine. Cover again with the foil; cook for 15 minutes. Place the tray of seasoned bread in the oven; bake for 10 minutes or until golden, turning halfway through the cooking time.

5 Let the mussels stand, covered, for 5 minutes. Remove any mussels that didn't open. Remove the foil, add the spinach, and toss to combine. Serve the tray bake topped with the toasted bread crumbs and the extra parsley sprigs.

Zucchini kaftas with smoky tomato aioli

VEGETARIAN | PREP + COOK TIME **45 MINUTES** | SERVES **4**

PER SERVING | Calories 505 | Carbohydrates 33g | Total sugars 4.5g | Fat 38g | Saturated fat 3.5g | Sodium 0.3g plus seasoning | Fiber 4g

For a relaxed lunch or picnic, serve the kaftas stuffed into whole-wheat pita pockets with a bitter green salad dressed with lemon juice, or pair them with one of the other vegetarian recipes in this chapter as part of a mezze spread.

½ lb (225g) Yukon gold potatoes, scrubbed, halved

1 lb (500g) zucchini, coarsely grated

1 long green chile, finely chopped

4 green onions, finely chopped

½ cup rice flour

sunflower oil, for frying

salt and freshly ground black pepper

micro sorrel or other soft-leaf herb, to garnish

smoky tomato aioli

2 tbsp chopped sun-dried tomatoes

1 chipotle chile in adobo sauce

1 garlic clove, chopped

½ cup mayonnaise

1 Put the potatoes in a small saucepan; cover with water. Bring to a boil; cook for 25 minutes or until tender. Drain, return to the pan, and coarsely mash with a fork.

2 Meanwhile, to make the smoky tomato aioli, put the sun-dried tomatoes in a small bowl; cover with boiling water. Let stand to plump up for 15 minutes; drain. Stir in the remaining aïoli ingredients until combined (or blend until smooth); season with salt and pepper to taste.

3 Place the grated zucchini in a clean dish towel or cheesecloth; twist the ends together, and squeeze over the sink to remove any excess moisture. Put the zucchini in a large bowl; add the mashed potato, chile, green onions, and rice flour. Season with salt and pepper to taste; mix well to combine.

4 Heat enough sunflower oil to reach a depth of ¼ inch (2cm) in a large frying pan over high heat. Shape ¼-cup measures of the zucchini mixture into ovals to make 12 kaftas in total. Fry them, in batches, for 3 minutes on each side or until golden and crisp. Remove with a slotted spoon; drain on paper towels.

5 Scatter the kaftas with the micro sorrel; serve with the aioli.

TIP

You can substitute ½ teaspoon smoked paprika and a pinch of chili powder for the chipotle chile in adobo sauce used in the aioli.

Indian-roasted chile, tomato, and chickpeas

VEGETARIAN | PREP + COOK TIME **30 MINUTES** | SERVES **4**

PER SERVING | Calories 387 | Carbohydrates 22g | Total sugars 6g | Fat 27g | Saturated fat 5g | Sodium 0.8g plus seasoning | Fiber 6.5g

Along with being rich in plant protein, chickpeas pack a pretty powerful nutritional punch for such unassuming-looking seeds. They provide slow-release, low-GI carbohydrates, stacks of fiber, essential minerals, and beneficial plant chemicals.

1 x 15 oz (425g) can chickpeas, drained, rinsed

6 long red chiles

1$^{1}/_{2}$ tsp brown mustard seeds

2 tsp cumin seeds

$^{1}/_{2}$ tsp dried chili flakes

2 tsp ground turmeric

$^{1}/_{3}$ cup extra virgin olive oil

2 tbsp curry leaves, plus extra 3 sprigs

1 lb (500g) cherry tomatoes

8 ready-to-cook papadams

$^{1}/_{2}$ cup Greek yogurt

salt and freshly ground black pepper

1 Preheat the oven to 400°F (200°C). Line a large baking sheet with parchment paper.

2 Line another large sheet with paper towels. Spread the chickpeas on the paper towels to absorb any excess moisture.

3 Cut the chiles in half lengthwise, keeping the stalk attached; remove and discard the seeds. Combine the mustard, cumin seeds, chili flakes, turmeric, olive oil, and curry leaves in a large bowl. Add the chiles, chickpeas, and tomatoes. Season with salt and pepper to taste; toss gently to combine.

4 Spread out the mixture over the parchment-lined baking sheet. Top with the extra sprigs of curry leaves. Bake, turning occasionally, for 15 minutes or until the tomatoes collapse and the chiles are tender.

5 Meanwhile, cook the papadams according to the package instructions.

6 Swirl a little of the tomato cooking juices through the yogurt. Serve the chickpea mixture with the yogurt sauce and papadams.

Golden cauliflower paella

HIGH-PROTEIN | PREP + COOK TIME **45 MINUTES** | SERVES **6**

PER SERVING | Calories 314 | Carbohydrates 22g | Total sugars 12g | Fat 8g | Saturated fat 1.5g | Sodium 2.2g plus seasoning | Fiber 9g

Cauliflower replaces white rice in this dish for a lower-carbohydrate version of paella.
A mix of seafood that includes fish, shrimp, and octopus will provide good levels of the
long-chain omega-3 fats that are anti-inflammatory and therefore can be helpful in relieving
all sorts of inflammatory conditions.

3 lb (1.5kg) cauliflower, cut into florets

3/4 lb (300g) red bell peppers, seeded

2 tbsp extra virgin olive oil

1/2 lb (225g) shallots, halved

1 tsp ground turmeric

1 tsp smoked paprika

2 cups chicken stock

1 x 15 oz (425g) can of chickpeas, drained, rinsed

12 oz (300g) raw shrimp, peeled, tails intact

8 oz (225g) raw calamari rings

4 oz (100g) uncooked octopus pieces

1/2 lb (225g) skinless firm white fish fillets, cut into chunks

8 oz (225g) cherry tomatoes

1/3 cup finely chopped flat-leaf parsley

salt and freshly ground black pepper

1 medium lemon, cut into wedges, for serving

chargrilled bread, for serving (optional)

1 In a food processor, pulse the cauliflower in batches until it has the consistency of coarse breadcrumbs. Thinly slice half of the red bell pepper; chop the remaining red bell pepper into 1/2 inch (1cm) pieces.

2 Heat the olive oil in a 10 inch (25cm) deep oven-proof skillet or paella pan over medium-high heat. Cook the shallots and chopped red pepper, stirring occasionally, for 5 minutes or until they start to brown and soften.

3 Add the cauliflower, turmeric, and smoked paprika; season with salt and pepper to taste. Cook, stirring continuously, for 2 minutes or until the cauliflower is heated through. Add the chicken stock, chickpeas, and sliced red pepper; cook, without stirring, for 10 minutes.

4 Add the seafood, fish, and tomatoes to the surface of the cauliflower mixture, pushing any large pieces of seafood into the mixture to submerge slightly. Cook for 5 minutes or until the liquid has been absorbed and the seafood is cooked through. Remove from the heat; allow the paella to stand for 5 minutes.

5 Sprinkle the paella with the parsley. Serve straight from the pan with the lemon wedges for squeezing over and the chargrilled bread for mopping up juices, if you like.

TIP

It is best to cook a paella over 2 burners so that heat is evenly distributed.

Pork with fennel and apple hash browns

HIGH-PROTEIN | PREP + COOK TIME **40 MINUTES** | SERVES **4**

PER SERVING | Calories 541 | Carbohydrates 44g | Total sugars 23g | Fat 21g | Saturated fat 4g | Sodium 0.6g plus seasoning | Fiber 10g

Pork is, strictly speaking, a red meat; however, nutritionally its profile is closer to white meat. Although it is perceived as being a fatty meat, pork breeding has changed in recent years and in fact most pork today is pretty lean. It is also rich in thiamine, which plays an essential role in metabolism.

⅓ cup extra virgin olive oil, divided

2 tbsp apple cider vinegar

2 tbsp whole-grain mustard

2 tbsp honey

1¼ lb (600g) pork tenderloin

1¼ lb (600g) fennel, trimmed, fronds reserved, divided

¾ lb (350g) Russet potatoes

¾ lb (350g) Gala or Fuji apples, halved, cored, divided

¼ cup whole-wheat flour

¼ lb (100g) red cabbage, finely shredded

salt and freshly ground black pepper

1 Put 2 tablespoons of the olive oil, along with the vinegar, whole-grain mustard, and honey in a small jar with a leak-proof cap. Shake until well combined. Put ¼ cup of the dressing and the pork in a bowl. Season with salt and pepper to taste; toss to coat the pork evenly with the dressing.

2 To make the hash browns, coarsely grate the fennel, potato, and 1 of the apples. Combine the grated mixture in a clean cheese cloth; twist the ends of the cheese cloth and squeeze firmly over the sink to remove any excess liquid. Transfer the mixture to a large bowl, stir in the flour and 1 tablespoon chopped fennel fronds; season with salt and pepper to taste. Shape the mixture into 4 flat patty shapes.

3 Heat the remaining olive oil in a large nonstick skillet over medium-high heat. Cook the hash browns for 4 minutes on each side or until golden brown.

4 Meanwhile, preheat a medium nonstick frying pan over high heat. Cook the pork for 4 minutes on each side or until browned and cooked to the desired temperature. Allow the pork to rest, covered, in the pan for 2 minutes. Transfer any pan juices to a small bowl for serving.

5 Slice the remaining apple thinly; toss with the cabbage and remaining dressing. Serve the sliced pork and hash browns with the salad and any pan juices, topped with the remaining fennel fronds.

Braised balsamic lentils and butternut squash

VEGETARIAN | PREP + COOK TIME **1 HOUR 25 MINUTES** | SERVES **4**

PER SERVING | Calories 411 | Carbohydrates 47g | Total sugars 26g | Fat 15g | Saturated fat 6g | Sodium 0.6g plus seasoning | Fiber 14g

Pulses contain phytates. Although these have received some bad press, mostly on account of their ability to bind minerals such as iron, lowering absorption, overall phytates have been associated with beneficial effects. By consuming a varied diet with plenty of foods rich in minerals, you need not be concerned.

1½ lb (1.5kg) whole butternut squash, washed

2 tbsp extra virgin olive oil

¾ lb (350g) carrots, cut into large pieces

¼ lb (100g) shallots, peeled

8 sprigs of thyme, divided

6 garlic cloves, unpeeled

1 cup vegetable stock

1 x 14 oz (397g) can brown lentils, drained, rinsed

¼ cup caramelized balsamic vinegar

4 oz (120g) goat milk yogurt

salt and freshly ground black pepper

1 Preheat the oven to 400°F (200°C).

2 Cut the butternut squash in half lengthwise, cutting from the base through to the stalk end. (Take care, as the stalk end is particularly hard.) Using a metal spoon, remove and discard the seeds. Make 4 cuts widthwise, taking the knife blade three-quarters of the way down into the flesh of each squash half, without reaching the skin.

3 Place the squash halves, cut-side up, in a deep roasting pan just large enough to fit the ingredients (if it's too big, the ingredients will evaporate too quickly). Season generously with salt and pepper; drizzle with the olive oil. Add the carrots, shallots, 6 of the thyme sprigs, and garlic to the pan. Combine the vegetable stock with ½ cup water and pour over top. Cover the pan tightly with 2 layers of aluminum foil.

4 Bake the butternut squash for 45 minutes until just tender (depending on the thickness of the squash, it may require an additional 10 minutes). Remove the pan from the oven. Uncover carefully and sprinkle the lentils over top. Drizzle with the balsamic vinegar.

5 Increase the oven temperature to 425°F (220°C). Roast the squash and lentils, uncovered, for 15 minutes longer or until the squash flesh is starting to brown and the braising liquid has reduced in volume by half.

6 Meanwhile, make goat curd by straining the yogurt through cheese cloth in a strainer placed over a bowl. Let all the liquid drain.

7 Serve the roasted vegetables and lentils topped with the goat curd and remaining 2 sprigs of thyme.

TIP

Make sure the roasting pan is just large enough to fit the ingredients. If it's too large, the liquid will evaporate too quickly.

Swiss chard dolmades

VEGETARIAN | PREP + COOK TIME **55 MINUTES** | SERVES **4**

PER SERVING | Calories 682 | Carbohydrates 70g | Total sugars 19g | Fat 31g | Saturated fat 13g | Sodium 3.3g plus seasoning | Fiber 9g

Two of the world's healthiest diets, the Mediterranean and the Okinawan, have in common their frequent consumption of dark leafy greens. Leafy greens are fabulous foods to eat every day. Low in calories and carbs, they have almost no effect on blood glucose.

3 cups cooked brown rice

8 oz (225g) fresh firm ricotta cheese

2 tsp finely grated lemon zest

1/2 tsp ground cinnamon

2 tbsp chopped fresh dill, divided,
plus extra sprigs, to garnish

2 tbsp currants

8 oz (225g) feta cheese, crumbled, divided

1 lb (480g) Swiss chard (at least 8 large leaves),
stems removed

2 x 14 oz (792g) jars spicy pasta sauce

7 oz (200g) whole-wheat sourdough bread,
coarsely chopped

2 tbsp extra virgin olive oil

salt and freshly ground black pepper

1 Preheat the oven to 400°F (200°C).

2 Put the rice in a large bowl with the ricotta cheese, lemon zest, cinnamon, 2 tablespoons chopped dill, currants, and 4 oz (112g) of the feta cheese. Season with salt and pepper to taste.

3 Place the Swiss chard leaves side by side on a clean work surface. Divide the rice mixture evenly among the chard leaves, placing it at one end of each leaf. Roll up the leaves tightly, folding in the sides as you roll. Arrange the dolmades side by side in a 9 x 13 inch (21cm x 32cm) oven-safe dish. Pour the pasta sauce over top.

4 In a food processor, pulse the bread until coarse crumbs form. Toss the crumbs with the olive oil to combine; sprinkle over the top of the dolmades with the remaining feta cheese. Bake for 30 minutes—covering with aluminum foil halfway through the cooking time if the feta cheese is browning too quickly—or until the crumbs and feta cheese are golden. Serve topped with the extra dill sprigs.

TIPS

• Instead of a spicy pasta sauce, you can use a mild variety if you like.

• For even cooking, make sure to select 8 large Swiss chard leaves that are equal in size.

Lentil and vegetable stuffed tomatoes

VEGETARIAN | PREP + COOK TIME **40 MINUTES** | SERVES **4**

PER SERVING | Calories 402 | Carbohydrates 22g | Total sugars 15g | Fat 25g | Saturated fat 9g | Sodium 1.3g plus seasoning | Fiber 10g

Both the lentils and walnuts in this recipe contribute fiber and protein. Walnuts are an impressive source of plant omega-3 fat alpha–linolenic acid (ALA), with 1 ounce (30g) of walnuts providing 1.9g of it. ALA cannot be made in the body and must be obtained from our diet. It seems to play a role in heart health.

3¹/₂lb (1.8kg) large vine tomatoes

³/₄lb (350g) fennel bulb, trimmed, fronds reserved

1 x 14 oz (397g) can brown lentils, drained, rinsed

2 garlic cloves, crushed

¹/₄ cup finely chopped fresh dill

1 tsp ground cumin

1 tsp dried mint

¹/₂ cup coarsely chopped roasted walnuts

8 oz (225g) firm feta cheese, cut into 1 in (2.5cm) cubes

2 tbsp extra virgin olive oil

1 tsp finely grated lemon zest, to garnish

salt and freshly ground black pepper

1   Preheat the oven to 425°F (220°C). Line a baking sheet with parchment paper.

2   Slice the tops off the tomatoes; reserve. Using a small spoon, scoop out the flesh from each tomato; reserve ¹/₄ cup tomato pulp. Place the tomatoes on the parchment-lined baking sheet.

3   Trim ¹/₃ cup fronds from the fennel bulb; reserve. Chop the remaining fronds. Slice the fennel stalks into rounds; cut the bulb into wedges. In a large bowl, combine the lentils, garlic, dill, chopped fennel fronds, cumin, mint, walnuts, and reserved tomato pulp. Mix well; season with salt and pepper to taste.

4   Spoon the lentil mixture into each tomato cavity, pressing down firmly; cover with the reserved tomato tops. Place the fennel slices and wedges with the feta cheese on the baking sheet between the tomatoes. Drizzle with half of the olive oil. Season with salt and pepper to taste. Bake for 15 minutes or until the tomatoes are tender.

5   Remove the tomatoes from the oven; cover to keep warm. Continue to bake the fennel and feta cheese for 15 minutes longer or until golden brown. Return the tomatoes to the tray; sprinkle with the lemon zest and the reserved fennel fronds. Drizzle with the remaining olive oil.

Roasted Mexican chicken

HIGH-PROTEIN | PREP + COOK TIME **1 HOUR 5 MINUTES** | SERVES **4**

PER SERVING | Calories 490 | Carbohydrates 41g | Total sugars 13g | Fat 12g | Saturated fat 3g | Sodium 0.8g plus seasoning | Fiber 11g

Using skinless chicken legs helps to reduce the fat content of this dish. It also allows the chicken legs to absorb the smoky herbs and spices more readily, upping the intensity of the flavors. Serve with light sour cream, if you like.

1 1/2 lb (750g) chicken legs, skin removed (see tip)

2 tsp smoked paprika

2 tsp ground coriander

1 tbsp extra virgin olive oil

1 x 14 oz (396g) jar spicy pasta sauce

2 cups chicken stock

1/2 cup brown basmati rice

1 x 15 1/2 oz (439g) can red kidney beans, drained, rinsed

2 red bell peppers, quartered, stems left intact

1/2 cup red onion, cut into wedges

salt and freshly ground black pepper

1 cup cilantro, to garnish

lime wedges, for serving

1   Preheat the oven to 350°F (180°C).

2   Coat the chicken in the combined smoked paprika and ground coriander. Heat the oil in a large flameproof roasting pan or casserole dish. Brown the chicken for 3 minutes on each side or until lightly golden.

3   Add the pasta sauce, stock, rice, kidney beans, red peppers, and onion to the pan. Season with salt and pepper to taste; bring to a simmer.

4   Transfer to the oven; bake, covered, for 30 minutes. Remove the lid; cook, uncovered, for 10 minutes longer or until the chicken is cooked through and the rice is tender. Let stand for 5 minutes; serve topped with the cilantro and with lime wedges for squeezing over.

TIP

Removing the skin from the chicken legs keeps the fat content low in this recipe. You can instead use skinless chicken thighs.

Cumin lamb with beet and feta cheese salad

HIGH-PROTEIN | PREP + COOK TIME **30 MINUTES** | SERVES **6**

PER SERVING | Calories 508 | Carbohydrates 20g | Total sugars 14g | Fat 30g | Saturated fat 11g | Sodium 1.3g plus seasoning | Fiber 5.5g

Red meat is a fabulous source of high-quality protein. Research has shown pretty conclusively that high-protein diets help us to control our weight and, most importantly, keep off any lost weight. Always choose good-quality red meat and limit how much of it you eat.

1¼ lb (800g) lamb loin chops

¼ cup extra virgin olive oil, divided

1 tbsp honey

2 tsp cumin seeds, toasted

1 lb (500g) cooked baby beets (see tip)

1 x 14 oz (397g) can brown lentils, drained, rinsed

¼ cup balsamic vinegar

¼ lb (120g) red cabbage, thinly sliced

8 oz (225g) firm feta cheese

8 green onions

⅓ cup coarsely chopped walnuts, toasted, for serving

salt and freshly ground black pepper

1 Preheat a ridged cast-iron grill pan or heavy skillet over high heat.

2 Combine the lamb, 1 tablespoon of the olive oil, the honey, and the cumin in a bowl; season. Let stand for 15 minutes.

3 Put the beets, lentils, vinegar, and remaining olive oil in a bowl; season with salt and pepper to taste. Toss well to coat. Arrange the cabbage on a platter with the beet and lentil mixture.

4 Pat the feta cheese dry between layers of paper towels. Place the feta cheese directly in the grill pan. Cook for 3 minutes or until grill marks appear and the feta cheese starts to brown around the edges. Using a wide spatula, carefully turn the feta cheese over; cook for 3 minutes longer or until charred. Remove the feta cheese from the pan and place it on the salad.

5 Meanwhile, cook the lamb on the ridged grill pan for 3 minutes on each side or until cooked to your liking. Transfer to a plate; let the lamb rest, loosely covered with foil. Grill the green onions for 2 minutes on each side or until just softened and charred. Slice the lamb; serve with the salad, green onions, and chopped walnuts.

TIP

To roast 1 bunch of fresh baby beets, trim the stems and scrub. Wrap the beets in aluminum foil. Roast at 400°F (200°C) for 40 minutes or until tender; cool, then peel.

Ginger-roasted sea trout with pickled beet and couscous

FAST | PREP + COOK TIME **25 MINUTES** | SERVES **4**

PER SERVING | Calories 436 | Carbohydrates 26g | Total sugars 15g | Fat 15g | Saturated fat 1g | Sodium 0.7g plus seasoning | Fiber 6g

The punchy flavors in this citrusy marinade would work well with other oily fish such as salmon, mackerel, or sardines. You can replace the trout with salmon fillets, if you like. Keep the skin on for cooking; it helps keep the fish moist. You can always peel it off afterward.

½ lb (200g) beets

2 tbsp white balsamic vinegar

pinch of salt

2 oranges

1 tbsp grated fresh ginger

2 tsp cumin seeds

2 tbsp extra virgin olive oil, divided

1¾ lb (800g) sea trout fillets (in 4 fillets), skin on

¾ cup whole-wheat couscous

⅓ cup coarsely chopped flat-leaf parsley

¾ lb (350g) watercress, trimmed

salt and freshly ground black pepper

1 Preheat the oven to 350°F (180°C). Line a baking sheet with parchment paper.

2 Peel the beets. Using a mandoline, V-slicer, or wide vegetable peeler, shave them into rounds. Place in a bowl with the balsamic vinegar and a pinch of salt; set aside until needed.

3 To make the marinade, finely grate 2 teaspoons of zest from one of the oranges into a small bowl. Squeeze the juice from 1 orange. Add 2 tablespoons to the same bowl; reserve the remaining juice. Next, add the ginger, cumin, and 1 tablespoon of the olive oil; season with salt and pepper to taste. Cut the zest and white pith from the remaining orange, then use a sharp knife to slice the orange into ¼ inch (6mm) round slices. Cut each slice in half; set aside for serving.

4 Score 2 slits about ¾ in (2cm) deep lengthwise into the skin side of the fish fillets. Rub half of the marinade all over the fish and into the slits; place on the prepared baking sheet, skin side up, and spoon over the remaining marinade. Bake the fish for 10 minutes or until just cooked through.

5 Meanwhile, put the couscous in a large heatproof bowl; pour ¾ cup boiling water over it and cover. Let stand for 5 minutes; fluff the grains with a fork. Toss through the parsley and 2 tablespoons of the reserved orange juice; season with salt and pepper to taste.

6 Spoon the couscous onto a platter; add the watercress, drained pickled beets, and orange slices. Drizzle with the remaining olive oil. Top with the trout fillets, drizzling over any pan juices, and serve.

SWEET

Indulging a sweet tooth need not mean
abandoning healthier eating for culinary sin.
Special indulgences, fruit-filled goodness,
treats for mid-afternoon snacks—all are
found here.

Red velvet waffles

GLUTEN-FREE | PREP + COOK TIME **45 MINUTES** | MAKES **8**

PER SERVING | Calories 289 | Carbohydrates 27g | Total sugars 19g | Fat 15g | Saturated fat 2g | Sodium 0.5g | Fiber 3g

The berries in the compote are high in vitamin C and contain many potentially beneficial plant chemicals that have been shown to have antiviral and antibacterial properties. The beet in the waffles is a great source of fiber, minerals, and vitamin C.

$\frac{1}{4}$ cup cocoa powder

$\frac{1}{2}$ cup masa harina (see tips)

1$\frac{3}{4}$ cups almond flour

1 tsp baking soda

2 cups beet, finely grated

1 cup buttermilk

1 tsp vanilla extract

2 tbsp honey

2 eggs, separated

olive oil cooking spray

powdered sugar, for serving (optional)

berry compote

$\frac{1}{4}$ cup honey

2 tsp vanilla extract

16 oz (550g) frozen mixed berries, thawed

1 Sift the cocoa, masa, almond flour, and baking soda into a large bowl, stirring the mixture to combine. Add the grated beet, buttermilk, vanilla, honey, and egg yolks; mix to combine.

2 Using a mixer, whip the egg whites with a pinch of salt until stiff peaks form. Gently fold the whites into beet mixture; let stand for 10 minutes.

3 Meanwhile, to make the berry compote, heat the honey and vanilla in a large frying pan over high heat until boiling. Add the berries; cook, stirring, for 4 minutes or until the juices release.

4 Grease a waffle iron with cooking spray; heat according to the manufacturer's instructions. Working in batches, add $\frac{1}{3}$ cup batter to the waffle iron; cook for 3 minutes or until cooked through. Remove and set aside to keep warm. Repeat with the remaining batter to make a total of 8 waffles.

5 Serve the waffles topped with the berry compote and, if desired, dusted with powdered sugar.

TIPS

- Masa harina is finely ground cornmeal; look for it in the grocery aisle with specialty grains and flours.
- You can swap out the almond flour for the same amount of hazelnut meal.

Banoffee mousse pots

FAST | PREP + COOK TIME **15 MINUTES + FREEZING** | SERVES **6**
PER SERVING | CALORIES 688 | Carbohydrates 77g | Total sugars 62g | Fat 37g | Saturated fat 26g | Sodium 0.4g | Fiber 5g

Banoffee pie, a traditional British treat, is a mixture of banana and toffee flavors in a sweet
custard pie. We've reworked the original recipe using coconut cream instead of cream.
The natural sweetness of dates replaces sweetened condensed milk.

2 x 13½ oz (400ml) cans coconut milk with
coconut cream, refrigerated (see tips)

3 lb (1.4 kg) bananas, divided

1 tbsp honey, plus extra, for serving (optional)

1 tsp vanilla extract

1 cup firmly packed pitted fresh dates

¼ cup smooth natural peanut butter

½ tsp ground cinnamon

¼ tsp sea salt flakes

2 oz (55g) dark chocolate (70% cocoa),
coarsely chopped

1   Scoop the thick cream off the top of both cans of coconut milk.
You will need 2 cups of it. Reserve the remaining liquid.

2   Peel 5 of the bananas; in the bowl of a food processor, combine them
with the thick coconut cream, honey, and vanilla . Process until
completely smooth. Divide evenly among six 1-cup glasses. Place on
a tray and freeze for 1 hour.

3   Meanwhile, in the bowl of a food processor, combine ¾ cup of the
reserved coconut liquid with the dates, peanut butter, cinnamon, and
salt. Process until completely smooth. Divide the mixture evenly over
the semi-set mousse pots. Return to the freezer for 1 hour or until
slightly firm.

4   Peel the remaining banana; cut diagonally into small pieces. Top the
mousse pots with the banana and the chopped chocolate. Drizzle with
extra honey, if you like.

TIPS

- For this recipe, avoid light coconut milk since
the cream will have been removed.
- If you freeze the mousse pots for longer than
1 hour, thaw them at room temperature for
25 minutes before serving.

Blueberry and ricotta hand pies

MAKE-AHEAD/PORTABLE | PREP + COOK TIME **55 MINUTES** | SERVES **6**

PER SERVING | Calories 355 | Carbohydrates 35g | Total sugars 15g | Fat 19g | Saturated fat 4g | Sodium 0.1g | Fiber 3g

Oozing with creaminess laced with concentrated bursts of berry goodness, these hand pies are not as sinful a treat as you might think. For just a bit more of a flavor hit, serve them dusted with confectioner's sugar and topped with extra strips of lemon zest, if you like.

$1^1/_4$ cup whole-wheat flour

$^1/_3$ cup almond meal

$^1/_3$ cup palm sugar, divided, plus extra 2 tsp, for sprinkling

8 oz (225g) ricotta cheese

$^1/_4$ cup extra virgin olive oil

8 oz (225g) blueberries

1 tbsp finely grated lemon zest

2 tbsp lemon juice

1 tbsp corn starch

1 egg, lightly beaten

1 Preheat the oven to 350°F (180°C). Line a baking sheet with parchment paper.

2 In the bowl of a food processor, combine the whole-wheat flour, almond meal, and 2 teaspoons of the $^1/_3$ cup palm sugar. Process until combined. Add the ricotta cheese, olive oil, and 2 tablespoons ice-cold water; pulse until the dough starts to come together. Transfer to a work surface and gently knead to bring the dough together. Cut the dough in half, shape each half into a disc, and wrap in plastic wrap. Leave to chill in the fridge for 30 minutes.

3 Meanwhile, put the blueberries, remaining palm sugar, lemon zest, lemon juice, and corn starch in a medium saucepan. Cook, stirring and lightly crushing some of the berries, over medium heat for 4 minutes or until the mixture thickens. Transfer to a bowl; cool slightly.

4 Roll out half of the dough to $^1/_{16}$ inch (2mm) thick on a lightly floured surface. Using a $3^1/_2$ inch (9cm) cutter, cut out six rounds. Place on the prepared baking sheet. Divide the berry filling evenly among the rounds, leaving a $^1/_2$ inch (1cm) border around the edges. Lightly brush the edges of the dough with the beaten egg. Roll out the remaining dough on a lightly floured surface; cut out six 4 inch (10.5cm) rounds. Cover the pies with the larger rounds, pressing down on the edges with a fork to seal. Lightly brush the tops with more of the beaten egg and sprinkle with the extra palm sugar. Using a sharp knife, cut two $^3/_4$ inch (2cm) slashes in the top of each pie.

5 Bake for 25 minutes or until golden brown. Serve the hand pies warm or cold.

TIP

You can also make the hand pies using raspberries instead of blueberries, or use hazelnut meal in place of the almond meal.

15-minute strawberry and coconut sticky rice pudding

FAST | PREP + COOK TIME **15 MINUTES** | SERVES **4**

PER SERVING | Calories 695 | Carbohydrates 71g | Total sugars 25g | Fat 38g | Saturated fat 20g | Sodium 0.6g | Fiber 8g

Mango with sticky rice is a traditional and extremely popular sweet treat in Thailand and other parts of Southeast Asia such as Laos and Vietnam. Here it is given a less traditional treatment with brown rice in place of the usual glutinous rice. It's not an everyday treat because of the coconut cream, so save it for a special occasion.

3 cups cooked brown rice

1 x 13¹/₂ oz (400 ml) can coconut milk with coconut cream

³/₄ cup quinoa flakes

¹/₄ cup natural, unsweetened cashew butter

¹/₄ cup pure maple syrup, divided, plus extra 2 tbsp, for serving (see tips)

1 tsp ground cinnamon

pinch of sea salt flakes

1 lime

12oz (400g) strawberries

¹/₄ cup pistachios, coarsely chopped

1   In a large saucepan, combine the rice, coconut cream, quinoa flakes, cashew butter, 2 tbsp of the maple syrup, cinnamon, sea salt flakes, and 2 cups water. Cook over medium-high heat, stirring continuously, for 10 minutes or until the mixture has a soft, creamy texture.

2   Meanwhile, finely grate 1 teaspoon of zest from the lime; reserve. Squeeze 1 tablespoon of juice from the lime. Put 12 oz (300g) of the strawberries in a small saucepan with the remaining maple syrup and the lime juice. Cook, stirring, over medium-high heat for 10 minutes or until it has thickened slightly and the strawberries have broken down.

3   Top the hot rice pudding with the warm strawberry compote, remaining strawberries, pistachios, reserved lime zest, and the extra 2 tablespoons maple syrup to taste. Serve immediately.

TIPS

- Add the maple syrup to taste, depending on the sweetness of the strawberries.
- The pudding thickens on standing so, if reheating, stir in a little extra water to loosen.

Chocolate mousse with blackberries and hazelnut crunch

FAST | PREP + COOK TIME **20 MINUTES + REFRIGERATION** | SERVES **4**

PER SERVING | Calories 442 | Carbohydrates 31g | Total sugars 28g | Fat 27g | Saturated fat 9g | Sodium 0.3g | Fiber 6g

Chocolate does more than simply taste good and lift your mood. Not only is it packed with minerals and antioxidants, but it may help lower blood pressure and cholesterol. To get the full health benefits, use pure cocoa and dark chocolate with at least 70% cocoa solids.

½ cup hazelnuts

¼ cup pure maple syrup, divided

¼ cup coconut milk powder, divided

½ tsp sea salt flakes

1½ cups frozen blackberries

3½ oz (100g) dark chocolate (85% cocoa), chopped

10 oz (300g) silken tofu, drained

1   Preheat the oven to 350°F (180°C). Line a baking sheet with parchment paper.

2   On the baking sheet, toss the hazelnuts with 2 teaspoons of the maple syrup, 2 teaspoons of the coconut milk powder, and the sea salt. Bake for 8 minutes or until dark golden and caramelized. Let cool on the tray, then coarsely chop the resulting hazelnut crunch.

3   Meanwhile, put the blackberries in a small saucepan with 1 tablespoon of the maple syrup and 1 tablespoon water. Bring to a simmer; cook for 5 minutes or until the berries start to break down and release their juices. Refrigerate for 10 minutes.

4   Put the chocolate in a glass microwave-safe bowl. Microwave on high (100%) in 30-second increments, stirring between each one, until the chocolate is melted and smooth. Let cool for 5 minutes.

5   In the bowl of a food processor, combine the melted chocolate, tofu, remaining coconut milk powder, and remaining maple syrup. Process until very smooth.

6   Spoon three-quarters of the berry mixture into four 1-cup serving dishes or glasses. Top with the chocolate mousse mixture. Refrigerate for 4 hours or overnight. Spoon over the remaining berry mixture. Serve sprinkled with the hazelnut crunch.

Gluten-free pancakes with strawberries

GLUTEN-FREE | PREP + COOK TIME **45 MINUTES** | SERVES **8**

PER SERVING | Calories 252 | Carbohydrates 26g | Total sugars 12g | Fat 12g | Saturated fat 3g | Sodium 0.7g | Fiber 3g

Quinoa flour and almond flour replace refined white flour in this pancake recipe to make a more wholesome option that will suit people with celiac disease. To make the recipe dairy-free, too, swap the Greek yogurt for your favorite nondairy variety.

2 cups quinoa flour

3 tsp gluten-free baking powder

$^2/_3$ cup almond flour

2 cups almond milk

$^1/_3$ cup pure maple syrup, plus 1 extra tbsp, for serving

2 eggs, lightly beaten

extra virgin olive oil cooking spray

$^2/_3$ cup Greek yogurt

8oz (225g) strawberries, halved

1 Sift the quinoa flour and baking powder into a large bowl; stir in the almond flour.

2 Combine the almond milk, $^1/_3$ cup maple syrup, and beaten eggs in a small bowl. Stir into the dry ingredients until well combined.

3 Spray an 8 inch (20cm) nonstick skillet with olive oil, then heat over medium heat. Pour in $^1/_2$ cup of the batter; cook for 3 minutes or until bubbles appear on the surface. Turn; cook for 1 minute longer or until golden underneath. Remove from the pan; cover to keep warm. Repeat to make a total of 8 pancakes.

4 Top the pancakes with the yogurt and strawberries. Drizzle with the extra 1 tablespoon maple syrup, and serve.

Peach and yogurt tiramisu pots

FAST | PREP + COOK TIME **15 MINUTES** | SERVES **4**

PER SERVING | Calories 553 | Carbohydrates 57g | Total sugars 49g | Fat 27g | Saturated fat 14g | Sodium 0.4g | Fiber 5g

This healthier makeover of the classic tiramisu ditches mascarpone in favor of a mixture of lower-fat ricotta cheese and Greek yogurt. The addition of peaches contributes toward your daily fruit and vegetable intake.

10 oz (300g) ricotta cheese

1$\frac{1}{3}$ cups Greek yogurt, divided

2$\frac{1}{2}$ tbsp honey, divided

1 large orange

8 ladyfinger cookies

1$\frac{1}{2}$ oz (40g) dark chocolate (70% cocoa), finely grated

1$\frac{1}{4}$ lb (600g) peaches, halved, cut into wedges

2 tbsp pine nuts

1 In the bowl of a food processor, combine the ricotta cheese, $\frac{1}{3}$ cup of the yogurt, and 1 tablespoon of the honey. Process until smooth. Transfer to a bowl; fold in the remaining yogurt. Refrigerate until needed.

2 Using a zesting tool, remove the zest from the orange in long strips; reserve for serving (alternatively, you can finely grate the zest). Juice the orange; you will need $\frac{1}{3}$ cup of juice. Put the orange juice and 2 teaspoons of the honey in a bowl; whisk to combine.

3 Break each cookie into 3 pieces. Place 3 pieces into the bottom of each of four 1-cup glasses; drizzle with half of the orange mixture. Top with half of the ricotta cheese mixture. Sprinkle with half of the grated chocolate and peach wedges. Add a second layer using the remaining cookies, orange mixture, ricotta mixture, grated chocolate, and peach wedges.

4 Toss the pine nuts in the remaining honey. Microwave on high (100%) for 50 seconds or until the honey and pine nuts are golden.

5 Divide the hot caramelized pine nuts evenly over the tiramisu pots. Serve sprinkled with the reserved orange zest.

TIP

Use a rasp grater, if you have one, to grate the chocolate very finely.

Chocolate fudge pie with whole-wheat crust

DAIRY-FREE | PREP + COOK TIME **1 HOUR 30 MINUTES** | SERVES **10**

PER SERVING | Calories 485 | Carbohydrates 58g | Total sugars 28g | Fat 23g | Saturated fat 15g | Sodium 0.3g | Fiber 6g

This clever pie utilizes the natural sweetness of sweet potato and honey in place of refined sugar. The sweet potato also adds fiber and a good array of B vitamins and vitamin C, while hazelnuts provide predominantly monounsaturated fats.

2 lb (1kg) sweet potatoes, halved

2 eggs

7 oz (200g) dark chocolate (70% cocoa), melted, cooled

1/4 cup honey

2 tbsp whole-wheat flour

1 cup canned coconut milk

2 tsp vanilla extract

1 tsp Dutch-process cocoa powder

1 cup dairy-free coconut yogurt, for serving

whole-wheat pie crust

1/3 cup hazelnut meal

1/3 cup rolled (old-fashioned) oats

1 1/4 cup whole-wheat flour

1/4 cup coconut oil

pinch of salt

1 Preheat the oven to 425°F (220°C). Line a baking sheet with parchment paper. Place the sweet potato, cut-side down, on the tray. Bake 30 minutes or until tender. Let stand for 5 minutes to cool slightly.

2 Meanwhile, make the pie crust. In a food processor, combine the hazelnut meal, rolled oats, flour, coconut oil, and a pinch of salt; process until fine crumbs form. With the motor operating, gradually add 1/3 cup ice-cold water until just combined. Press the mixture into a 7 inch (18cm) round pie dish. Refrigerate for 15 minutes or until chilled. Line the pastry with a parchment paper circle. Fill with dried beans or rice. Prebake for 15 minutes. Remove the paper and beans; bake 5 minutes longer or until the pastry is crisp.

3 When the sweet potatoes are cool enough to handle, scoop the flesh into the bowl of a food processor. Add the eggs, cooled melted chocolate, honey, flour, coconut milk, and vanilla; process until smooth and combined. Pour the mixture into the prebaked pie crust.

4 Reduce the oven temperature to 350°F (180°C). Bake the pie for 40 minutes or until just set. Let stand for 10 minutes, then refrigerate until chilled.

5 Dust the pie with the cocoa powder and serve with the coconut yogurt.

TIP

Dutch-process cocoa powder is darker than natural cocoa powder and has a mellower flavor. It goes through an alkalizing process when it is being made, neutralizing the natural acidity of the cocoa beans.

Spiced date, ginger, and hazelnut pear cake

HEALTHY FATS/HIGH-FIBER | PREP + COOK TIME **1 HOUR** | SERVES **10**

PER SERVING | Calories 321 | Carbohydrates 37g | Total sugars 23g | Fat 15g | Saturated fat 2g | Sodium 0.6g | Fiber 4g

It's a myth that cooking with olive oil destroys its benefits. Extra virgin olive oil that is of good quality has a high smoke point of around 410°F (210°C), so it can be used for stir-fries, frying, roasting, and baking without degrading. Store your oil in a cool, dark place to retain its freshness and health-promoting properties.

3/4 cup hazelnuts

18 soft fresh dates, pitted, halved

1 tsp baking soda

1/3 cup extra virgin olive oil, plus extra for greasing

4 eggs

1 1/2 lb (200g) whole-wheat flour

1 tsp baking powder

1/2 tsp salt

2 tsp ground ginger

1/3 cup pure maple syrup, divided

1 1/4 lb (600g) pears

1 Preheat the oven to 350°F (180°C). Spray the insides of a 10 inch (25cm) springform pan with cooking spray. Line the bottom of the pan with parchment paper. Set aside.

2 Put the dates, baking soda, and 1/2 cup boiling water in a large heat-safe bowl; let stand for 5 minutes to soften. Place in the bowl of the food processor, and pulse the mixture until smooth.

3 In a large bowl, combine the date mixture, ground hazelnuts, olive oil, eggs, flour, ginger, and 1/4 cup of the maple syrup; mix until just combined. Peel and grate 1 of the pears; fold through the cake mixture.

4 Spoon the mixture into the prepared pan. Slice the remaining pears thinly using a mandoline or V-slicer. Arrange the pear slices on top of the cake. Brush with the remaining maple syrup.

5 Bake the cake for 50–60 minutes or until a toothpick inserted into the center comes out clean. Let the cake cool in the pan for 10 minutes before transferring to a wire rack to cool.

Easy fruit salads

Fruit salad is simple to make, and you can enjoy an almost endless array of taste sensations by choosing complementary combinations ranging from the classic to the exotic. Just be sure to select good-quality, perfectly ripe fruit for the best (and tastiest!) results.

Orange and rosemary

PREP + COOK TIME **15 MINUTES** | SERVES **4**

Remove the zest from 1 orange in long, thin strips using a zesting tool; reserve the zest and the orange. Remove and discard the peel and pith from 5 more oranges. Slice all the oranges crosswise into rounds. In a small bowl, combine the reserved zest strips, 1 cup sugar, $1/2$ cup water, and 2 small sprigs of rosemary in a large microwave-safe bowl; microwave on high (100%) for $2 1/2$ minutes or until the sugar dissolves and the syrup is hot. Carefully add this to the orange slices and 2 tablespoons lemon juice. Let cool for 10 minutes. Serve the fruit salad topped with 2 tablespoons crumbled pistachio halva and $1/2$ cup pomegranate seeds. (Tip: Halva is a confection made from sesame seeds and sugar; it's available from Middle Eastern grocers and in the specialty aisles of some supermarkets.)

Watermelon and lychee

PREP + COOK TIME **20 MINUTES** | SERVES **8**

Cut 3 lb (1.5kg) seedless watermelon into batons. Drain a 15 oz (426g) can of lychees. Place in a large bowl with 5 oz (150g) raspberries. Put $1 1/2$ cups sugar and $1 1/2$ cups water in a medium microwave-safe bowl; microwave on high (100%) for 3 minutes or until the sugar dissolves and the syrup is hot. Carefully remove the bowl from the microwave; add $1/4$ cup lime juice, 2 teaspoons finely grated lime zest, and 1 teaspoon vanilla extract. Cool the syrup mixture by stirring over a bowl of ice water. Pour the syrup mixture over the fruit. Serve topped with extra lime zest.

Cherry and kombucha

PREP + COOK TIME **20 MINUTES** | SERVES **4**

Remove the pits from $1/2$ lb (225g) fresh cherries; place the cherries in a large microwave-safe bowl with 1 cup lemon and ginger kombucha. Microwave on high (100%) for 2 minutes or until the cherries soften slightly, mashing the fruit slightly with a fork halfway through the cooking time. Stir in 2 teaspoons rosewater. Slice 1 lb (500g) strawberries into rounds; add to the cherry mixture with $1 1/2$ teaspoons grated lemon zest. Spoon the fruit salad into 4 small bowls or 1-cup dessert glasses; over top, pour an extra $2/3$ cup kombucha, evenly divided among the bowls. Top with lemon slices and serve immediately.

Mango and lime

PREP + COOK TIME **20 MINUTES** | SERVES **4**

Remove the cheeks from 4 chilled mangoes. Using a large spoon, scoop to remove the mango flesh in one piece. Cut the flesh lengthwise into slices; place in a large bowl. Grate 4 oz (100g) palm sugar into a small microwave-safe bowl; add $1/2$ cup water and 6 shredded fresh makrut lime leaves. Microwave on high (100%) for $1 1/2$ minutes or until the sugar dissolves. Add 1 teaspoon finely grated lime zest and $1/4$ cup lime juice. Pour the hot syrup over the mango; toss to combine. Serve the fruit salad topped with $1/2$ cup fresh or toasted flaked coconut.

Stone fruit cobbler

HIGH-FIBER | PREP + COOK TIME **1 HOUR 10 MINUTES** | SERVES **4**
PER SERVING | Calories 402 | Carbohydrates 40g | Total sugar 29g | Fat 20g | Saturated fat 6g | Sodium 0.3g | Fiber 4g

Using a variety of stone fruit in this cobbler lets you benefit from the unique properties of each type. Try to choose plums that are red-fleshed because they will contain more anthocyanins. These plant pigments have a high antioxidant activity that are of benefit to our immune systems. Stone fruits boast plenty of vitamin C, among other nutrients.

2 yellow nectarines

2 white peaches

2 small plums

$\frac{1}{4}$ cup pure maple syrup

$\frac{1}{2}$ tsp ground cinnamon

3 eggs

1 tbsp light brown sugar

2 tsp finely grated lemon zest

1 tsp vanilla extract

2 tbsp white spelt flour

3 tsp corn starch

$\frac{1}{3}$ cup almond meal

2 tbsp butter, melted, cooled

2 tbsp sliced natural almonds

sifted powdered sugar, to garnish (optional)

1 Preheat the oven to 350°F (180°C). Lightly grease a 6-cup shallow oval baking dish.

2 Halve the fruit; remove the pits. Cut the flesh into quarters. Put in a large bowl with the maple syrup and cinnamon; toss to combine. Add to the baking dish. Cover with aluminum foil and bake for 25 minutes or until the fruit starts to soften.

3 Meanwhile, whisk together the eggs, brown sugar, lemon zest, and vanilla in the medium bowl of an electric mixer, on high, for 5 minutes or until ribbons form when the beaters are lifted. Combine the spelt and corn starch, sift them over the egg mixture, then add the almond meal and cooled butter. Using a large metal spoon, incorporate the ingredients gently. (Be careful not to overmix.)

4 Remove the foil from the baking dish. Spoon the mixture evenly over the fruit; sprinkle with the sliced almonds. Bake the cobbler for 18 minutes or until lightly golden. Lightly dust with sifted powdered sugar, if you like.

TIP

You could use four 1$\frac{1}{4}$ cup ovenproof dishes to make individual cobblers, if you like.

Honey and pineapple granita with coconut yogurt

FAST | PREP + COOK TIME **15 MINUTES + FREEZING** | SERVES **4**

PER SERVING | Calories 331 | Carbohydrates 46g | Total sugars 46g | Fat 13g | Saturated fat 9g | Sodium 0.1g | Fiber 6g

Even the zest of lime has health benefits. The skin of citrus fruit contains the two antioxidants limonene and coumarin, which have been shown to stimulate a detoxification enzyme that in turn helps to rid the body of potentially carcinogenic compounds.

2$\frac{1}{2}$lb (1.2kg) ripe pineapple

2 limes

2 tbsp honey

1 cup dairy-free coconut yogurt

$\frac{1}{2}$ cup shredded coconut, toasted, to garnish

1   Trim the pineapple, discarding the top, base, and skin. Cut in half lengthwise; coarsely chop the flesh, including the core. You will need 1$\frac{1}{2}$lb (650g) pineapple flesh.

2   Finely grate the zest from 1 of the limes, then juice it. In a food processor, combine the pineapple, honey, 2 tablespoons lime juice, and 2 teaspoons lime zest; process until smooth.

3   Strain the mixture into a shallow 6 x 9 inch (15cm x 23cm) baking dish, pressing down firmly to extract all of the juice. Freeze the granita mixture for 2$\frac{1}{2}$ hours or until firm.

4   Using a metal fork, break up any ice crystals in the dish; return the granita to the freezer. Repeat the process every hour for 2 more hours or until the granita is the texture of snow.

5   Divide the coconut yogurt among 4 serving glasses; top evenly with the granita. Thinly slice the remaining lime; top the granita with the lime and toasted shredded coconut. Serve immediately.

TIP

If your pineapple is not overly sweet, you may need to add a little extra honey, to taste.

Polenta and ricotta cake with rosemary lemon syrup

GLUTEN-FREE | PREP + COOK TIME **50 MINUTES** | SERVES **10**

PER SERVING | Calories 362 | Carbohydrates 32g | Total sugars 24g | Fat 21g | Saturated fat 5g | Sodium 0.9g | Fiber 0g

Best made on the day of serving, this cake has a rich, yellow color and an appealing moist texture courtesy of the cornmeal. Because cornmeal and almond meal replace any flour, this is a gluten-free option. It sacrifices nothing when it comes to lemony zestiness.

2 lemons

³/₄ cup fresh ricotta cheese

¹/₂ cup honey

¹/₃ cup extra virgin olive oil, plus extra for greasing

1 tsp vanilla extract

4 eggs, separated

²/₃ cup white or yellow cornmeal

1½ cups almond meal

2 tsp gluten-free baking powder

pinch of salt

rosemary lemon syrup

¹/₃ cup honey

4 large sprigs rosemary

¹/₄ cup lemon juice

1 tsp vanilla extract

2 small lemons, thinly sliced into rounds

whipped lemon ricotta cheese

³/₄ cup reduced-fat ricotta cheese

1 tbsp lemon juice

1 tsp honey

TIP

To avoid a mess, set the cake on a cooling rack over a baking sheet before pouring the syrup.

1 Put the lemons in a saucepan; cover with water, and bring to a boil. Top the lemons with a lid or small plate to keep submerged. Reduce the heat to medium and simmer for 30 minutes or until tender. Drain. When the lemons are cool enough to handle, tear them open; discard any seeds.

2 Preheat the oven to 325°F (160°C). Spray a 10 inch (25cm) springform pan with cooking spray. Line the bottom with parchment paper.

3 Blend or process the lemons, ricotta cheese, honey, olive oil, vanilla, and egg yolks until smooth.

4 Combine the cornmeal, almond meal, and baking powder in a large bowl; stir in the lemon mixture. In a separate bowl, use an electric mixer to beat the eggs whites with a pinch of salt until soft peaks form; fold into the cornmeal mixture. Spoon into the prepared pan, then smooth the top.

5 Bake the cake in the oven for 50–55 minutes or until a toothpick inserted into the center comes out clean.

6 Meanwhile, make the rosemary lemon syrup and whipped lemon ricotta cheese. For the syrup, put the honey, rosemary sprigs, and ¹/₂ cup water in a small saucepan over high heat. Bring to a boil; cook for 4 minutes. Add the lemon juice, vanilla, and lemon slices; simmer for 2 minutes. For the whipped lemon ricotta, blend or process the ricotta, lemon juice, honey, and 2 tablespoons water until smooth. Refrigerate until needed.

7 Spoon half of the hot rosemary lemon syrup over the warm cake while still in the pan; let stand until cool. Transfer the cake to a plate, and serve with the remaining syrup and the whipped lemon ricotta cheese.

Chocolate crackles

FAST | PREP + COOK TIME **20 MINUTES + REFRIGERATION** | SERVES **10**

PER SERVING | Calories 220 | Carbohydrates 24g | Total sugars 10g | Fat 12g | Saturated fat 9g | Sodium 0g | Fiber 3g

It's not just your imagination—chocolate really can cheer you up! The carbohydrates present
in it raise levels of serotonin, the feel-good chemical in your brain, and chocolate contains
phenylethylamine, which acts as a mood elevator.

2 cups puffed brown rice

³/₄ cup raw buckwheat

1 cup shredded coconut

3¹/₂ oz (100g) dark chocolate (85% cocoa),
broken into chunks

¹/₄ cup coconut oil

2 tbsp honey

2 tbsp chia seeds

¹/₂ cup freeze-dried strawberries, crushed

1   Preheat the oven to 350°F (180°C). Line a baking sheet with parchment
    paper. Line 12 holes of a standard muffin tin with baking cups.

2   Spread the puffed rice and buckwheat on the lined baking sheet; bake
    for 4 minutes. Stir in the coconut; bake 5 minutes longer or until evenly
    toasted. Allow to cool to room temperature.

3   Meanwhile, put the chocolate, coconut oil, and honey in a medium
    saucepan; stir over low heat until melted and smooth.

4   Add the toasted dry ingredients and chia seeds to the chocolate mixture;
    stir to coat evenly. Spoon the mixture into the prepared baking cups.
    Sprinkle with the freeze-dried strawberries. Refrigerate the crackles
    for 30 minutes or until set.

TIPS

- Store these in the fridge for up to 3 days.
- For 24 smaller chocolate crackles, make
in batches in an 18-hole mini-muffin tin.

Mango and raspberry financier cake

DAIRY-FREE | PREP + COOK TIME **50 MINUTES** | SERVES **12**

PER SERVING | Calories 311 | Carbohydrates 18g | Total sugars 12g | Fat 22g | Saturated fat 3g | Sodium 0.1g | Fiber 2g

Financiers are little buttery almond cakes, but for this version we've made one large cake and reworked the recipe with olive oil instead of the traditional butter, and replaced and reduced the sugar by using maple syrup.

1¼ lb (600g) ripe mangoes

⅓ cup extra virgin olive oil

⅓ cup pure maple syrup, divided, plus extra for serving (optional)

4 eggs, separated

2 tsp vanilla extract

2½ cups almond meal

⅔ cup white spelt flour

1 tsp ground cinnamon

½ tsp baking powder

4 oz (125g) raspberries

⅓ cup natural sliced almonds

1 Preheat the oven to 350°F (180°C). Line a 9 x 9 inch (23cm x 23cm) baking dish with parchment paper.

2 Cut the cheeks from the mango; peel. Cut the flesh from around the pit and one cheek to yield 1¼ cups of firmly packed finely chopped mango. Slice the remaining mango cheek thinly; reserve.

3 In the bowl of the food processor, combine the mango, olive oil, maple syrup, egg yolks, and vanilla. Process until completely smooth.

4 Sift the almond meal, spelt flour, cinnamon, and baking powder into a large bowl. Stir in the mango mixture until half combined.

5 In a large, clean bowl, beat the egg whites and a pinch of salt with an electric mixer until soft peaks form. Fold the egg white through the mango mixture until no lumps remain. (Be careful not to overmix.) Pour the mixture into the prepared baking dish. Carefully smooth the surface of the mixture; top with the reserved sliced mango and half of the raspberries.

6 Bake for 35–40 minutes or until puffed and golden, and when a toothpick inserted into the center of the cake comes out with fine crumbs attached. Cool in the pan.

7 Serve the financier cake topped with the remaining raspberries, almonds, and extra maple syrup, if you like.

Conversion chart

A note on Australian measures

- One Australian metric measuring cup holds approximately 250ml.

- One Australian metric tablespoon holds 20ml.

- One Australian metric teaspoon holds 5ml.

- The difference between one country's measuring cups and another's is within a two- or three-teaspoon variance, and should not affect your cooking results.

- North America, New Zealand, and the United Kingdom use a 15ml tablespoon.

Using measures in this book

- All cup and spoon measurements are level.

- The most accurate way of measuring dry ingredients is to weigh them.

- When measuring liquids, use a clear glass or plastic jug with metric markings.

- We use large eggs with an average weight of 60g. Fruit and vegetables are assumed to be medium unless otherwise stated.

Dry measures

metric	imperial
15g	$1/2$oz
30g	1oz
60g	2oz
90g	3oz
125g	4oz ($1/4$lb)
155g	5oz
185g	6oz
220g	7oz
250g	8oz ($1/2$lb)
280g	9oz
315g	10oz
345g	11oz
375g	12oz ($3/4$lb)
410g	13oz
440g	14oz
470g	15oz
500g	16oz (1lb)
750g	24oz ($1 1/2$lb)
1kg	32oz (2lb)

Liquid measures

metric	imperial
30ml	1 fluid oz
60ml	2 fluid oz
100ml	3 fluid oz
125ml	4 fluid oz
150ml	5 fluid oz
190ml	6 fluid oz
250ml	8 fluid oz
300ml	10 fluid oz
500ml	16 fluid oz
600ml	20 fluid oz
1000ml (1 liter)	$1 3/4$ pints

Length measures

metric	imperial
3mm	$1/8$in
6mm	$1/4$in
1cm	$1/2$in
2cm	$3/4$in
2.5cm	1in
5cm	2in
6cm	$2 1/2$in
8cm	3in
10cm	4in
13cm	5in
15cm	6in
18cm	7in
20cm	8in
22cm	9in
25cm	10in
28cm	11in
30cm	12in (1ft)

Oven temperatures

The oven temperatures in this book are for conventional ovens; if you have a convection oven, decrease the temperature by 10–20 degrees.

°F (Fahrenheit)	°C (Celsius)
250	120
300	150
325	160
350	180
400	200
425	220
475	240

Index

Acknowledgments

DK would like to thank Sophia Young, Joe Reville, Amanda Chebatte, and Georgia Moore for their assistance in making this book.

The Australian Women's Weekly Test Kitchen in Sydney has developed, tested, and photographed the recipes in this book.